DEGAS

DEGAS

Patrick Bade

PORTLAND HOUSE
NEW YORK

This edition published by Portland House
distributed by Outlet Book Co Inc.
a Random House Company
225 Park Avenue South
New York, New York 10003

ISBN 0-517-05378-0

8 7 6 5 4 3 2 1

Printed and bound in Hong Kong

INTRODUCTION

The art dealer, Ambroise Vollard, once asked Degas why he never married. Degas replied, 'I, marry? Oh, I could never bring myself to do it. I would have been in mortal misery all my life for fear my wife might say, "That's a pretty thing" after I had finished a picture.'

Degas hated conventional prettiness and there is great irony in the fact that his dancers now adorn table mats, greetings cards and jigsaw puzzles and have, in fact, become harmless and pretty. It takes an effort of the imagination to understand why these images seemed so shocking and subversive to Degas' contemporaries. Even the critics sympathetic to his aims were shocked when Degas first exhibited the wax statuette, *Little Dancer Aged 14*, now so familiar in the several bronze versions which grace museums around the world. Paul Mantz wrote in the newspaper *Le Temps*:

Now that the piece is finished, let us admit right away that the result is almost frightening. One walks round and round this little dancer, and yet one is not touched. A lot of praise and a lot of blame will doubtless be given to this statuette, which we had heard about beforehand, but which is nevertheless a surprise in its out-and-out realism. The poor child is standing up, wearing a cheap gauze dress, with a blue ribbon round her waist and her feet shod in the soft slippers which are used for the most elementary dancing exercises. Is she working? Bending back from the waist, already looking rather tired, she is stretching her arms, which meet behind her back. Formidable because mindless, with animal effrontery she pushes forward a face which is more like a little muzzle – an appropriate word in the circumstances, for the poor child has begun her training as a *petit rat*. Why is she so ugly?

Degas, *Little Dancer Aged 14*, 1880–81. The Tate Gallery, London.

The most vivid descriptions which we have of Degas nearly all date from his old age. Indeed, Degas seems to have become old remarkably early. The sensitive and passionate young man revealed in his early letters and self-portraits soon disappeared behind a protective mask of cynicism and cantankerousness. As early as 1871, when Degas was only 37, Berthe Morisot's mother remarked that he seemed older than Berthe's father. His temper was legendary. The picture dealer, Durand-Ruel, who successfully handled Degas over a period of decades, said, 'The man's only pleasure was to quarrel. One always had to agree with him and give way to him.' Degas managed to quarrel with most of his friends and colleagues at one time or another; the affable Renoir, who was one of his greatest admirers, exclaimed, 'What a creature he was, that Degas! All his friends had to leave him; I was one of the last to go, but even I couldn't stay till the end.'

In anything concerning art Degas was demanding and utterly inflexible. Even taking snapshots of his friends was turned into an ordeal, as Daniel Halévy, son of Degas' childhood friend, Ludovic Halévy, described in his diary in 1895, 'Degas raised his voice, became dictatorial, gave orders that a lamp be brought into the little salon and that anyone who wasn't going to pose should leave. The dutiful part of the evening began. We had to obey Degas' fierce will, his artist's ferocity. All his friends speak of him with terror. If you invite him for the evening, you know what to expect: two hours of military obedience.' Halévy noted the contrast between his 'beautiful, sad, intimate voice' when in a good mood and the 'combative one which has now become almost like a challenge to a duel.'

Degas carefully cultivated an image as a fussy, misanthropic bachelor who hated children, animals, flowers and most of the things liked by other people. Vollard relates how he went to Degas to invite him to dinner –

'Certainly, Vollard,' he said, 'but listen: will you have a special dish without butter prepared for me? Mind you, no flowers on the table, and you must have dinner at half past seven sharp. I know you won't allow anybody to bring a dog. And if there are to be any women I hope they won't come reeking of perfume. How horrible all those odours are when there are so many things that smell really good, like toast – or even manure! Ah –' he hesitated, 'and very few lights. My eyes, you know, my poor eyes!'

Degas' friends were willing to put up with his fads and his frequent aggressiveness not only because of his genius but because they recognised the nobility of character that lay behind the prickly exterior. He was capable of displaying great wit and charm when he wished. The writer Paul Valéry frequently met Degas at the home of his old friend Henri Rouart and left a vivid account of his impact upon the company, 'Every Friday, Degas – faithful, scintillating, exasperating – was the life and soul of M. Rouart's dinner parties. He was a source of wit, terror and merriment. He probed, he mimicked, he poured forth jokes, stories, maxims and banter, revealing every aspect of the most intelligent injustice, the soundest taste, the narrowest yet most clear-sighted passion. He would disparage the literary world, the Academy, writers who affected aloofness, artists who were the latest thing; he would quote Saint-Simon, Proudhon, Racine, and the bizarre pronouncements of M. Ingres. I can almost hear him now. His host, who adored him, would listen with indulgent admiration, while other guests, young men, old generals, silent ladies, would vary in their enjoyment of the flights of irony, the aesthetic judgements and the bursts of violence that came from this marvellous deviser of epigrams.'

Degas' malicious *bons mots* were widely enjoyed and repeated. The American painter James McNeill Whistler based his own brand of insulting wit on that of Degas.

Degas was apparently the only person of whom the sharp-tongued Whistler was afraid and it was said of him that, in the presence of Degas, his conversation was 'distinguished by brilliant flashes of silence.'

Quite another side of Degas' personality is displayed in the letters which he wrote to close friends, such as the industrialist Henri Rouart and the sculptor Bartholomé. Here one sees, in addition to the wit, a tender solicitude for his friends' well-being and a vein of deep melancholy and pessimism which became more marked as the years went by.

A particularly revealing letter exists, written in 1890 to Evariste de Valernes, an artist friend of his youth:

I have been thinking constantly of you with the most affectionate feelings and yet I did not write to you, my dear de Valernes.

Once again I see you and your little studio, where I gave the impression of looking around too quickly. I see it again, as if it were in front of me . . .

Here I must ask your pardon for a matter which often comes up in your conversation and more often still in your thoughts: it is to have been – or to have seemed to be – hard with you during our long relationship to art.

I have been unusually so with myself; you must be fully aware of this, since you felt constrained to reproach me with it and to be surprised that I had so little confidence in myself.

I was, or I seemed to be, hard with everyone through a sort of passion for brutality, which came from my uncertainty and my bad humour. I felt myself so badly made, so badly equipped, so weak, whereas it seemed to me that my calculations on art were so right. I brooded against the whole world and against myself. I ask your pardon sincerely if, beneath the pretext of this

damned art, I have wounded your very intelligent and fine mind, perhaps even your heart . . .

There are many records of Degas' attempts to help other artists, such as the impoverished Gauguin, and also of his concern for his models.

Degas was a conservative revolutionary, a bourgeois to his finger-tips, whose chief delight was in breaking rules and shocking the bourgeoisie. He did not like to be called a revolutionary and when Ludovic Halévy's wife did so he answered passionately, 'Revolutionary! Don't say that . . . We are tradition itself. It cannot be said too often.' However, when it came to the conservative art establishment of his day, Degas was fiercely uncompromising, far more so, indeed, than his fellow painters Manet, Renoir and Monet. To the end of his days he firmly rejected all offers of official recognition or honours.

The contrast between Degas' bourgeois attitudes and reactionary politics on the one hand and his revolutionary art on the other was striking in nineteenth-century France, where progressive art was expected to go together with progressive political ideas. Pissarro, who was himself a committed anarchist and a firm believer in the related march of progress in art and politics, found it difficult to reconcile Degas' art with his political ideas. In 1891 he wrote of Degas to his son, 'How to understand him . . . such an anarchist! In art, of course, and without realizing it!'

In his personal life Degas was, in the words of André Lhote, like a 'disastrously incorruptable accountant.' He felt an intense sense of loyalty to his family and his class. It was bourgeois rectitude which caused Degas to make great sacrifices to help pay family debts in 1875 and then, three years later, to break with his brother Achille for divorcing his wife.

Although much of Degas' art depicts the working

classes, or at least working-class women, he had little sympathy for or understanding of any class other than his own. His interest in working-class women was the detached curiosity of an anthropologist studying the ways of a primitive tribe. In both his political and his artistic ideas, Degas was an elitist. He was against the idea of education or equal opportunities for the people: 'How infamous it is to talk of equality, since there will always be rich and poor! In the old days everyone stayed in his place and dressed according to his station; now the most insignificant grocer's boy reads his paper and dresses up like a gentleman . . . What an infamous century this is! . . . ' Art too was, in his opinion, for the chosen few: 'Is painting made to be seen? You must understand, one works for two or three living friends, and for others whom one hasn't met or who have died.'

The least attractive aspect of Degas' character was the virulent anti-semitism of his later years which led him to question the racial ancestry of his models and to throw out those suspected of sympathy with Dreyfus, the Jew whose case aroused so much controversy in late nineteenth-century France. Whilst there can be no justification for Degas' bigotry, it should be seen once again as the result of loyalty to his class and in the context of the extremely bitter Dreyfus Affair. Degas no doubt regarded the supporters of Dreyfus as subversives trying to undermine the hegemony of the bourgeois in French society.

Hilaire Germain Edgar De Gas (it was only later that he adopted the form 'Degas') was born in Paris on 19 July 1834, the eldest of five surviving children of a wealthy banker. Degas' father was half Italian and his mother a Creole from New Orleans. Throughout his early years he was in close contact with his extended family in Naples and New Orleans. Degas' beloved mother died in 1847 when he was 13, a fact which may have had some bearing on his inhibited relations with women later in life. He

went to school at the distinguished and exclusive Lycée Louis-le-Grand, where he would have received a thorough, if somewhat limited, classical education and where he met two boys who were to be amongst his closest friends later in life, Henri Rouart and Ludovic Halévy.

After graduating from the Lycée in 1853, Degas enrolled as a law student, but his interests lay elsewhere and he had already begun to make copies of drawings in the Print Room of the Louvre. In 1855, he began to study with the artist Louis Lamothe and entered the École des Beaux-Arts. Degas' formal studies were brief and the chief importance of Lamothe was that he was a former pupil of Ingres and no doubt helped to form Degas' passionate admiration for that artist. Degas was able to meet the great man himself through his family friends the Valpinçons, who owned Ingres' famous painting *La Baigneuse* which became known as *La Baigneuse de Valpinçon*. In later years, Degas gave varying accounts of the circumstances of his meeting with Ingres, but Ingres' exhortation to 'draw lines' was advice that he followed for the rest of his life. This enthusiasm for Ingres would have been unfashionable amongst the progressive artists of Degas' generation, who regarded him as a boring and reactionary painter.

Degas' love of Ingres did not prevent him from admiring his arch-rival Delacroix as well. He wished to combine the expressive qualities of Ingres' line and Delacroix's colour, and once said of himself, 'I am a colourist with line.' Although he was first and foremost a linear artist, Degas became a great colourist in the later years of his career. He was able to achieve this through the medium of pastel, which had a tremendously liberating effect on his use of colour in the late 1870s. The dichotomy of Degas' taste apparent in his enthusiasm for both Ingres and Delacroix was also reflected in his love of a wide range of old masters both linear and painterly.

Early copies and notebooks show his interest in Giotto, Fra Angelico, Signorelli, Raphael, Holbein, Cranach, Veronese, Poussin, Rembrandt and many others. In 1874, Edmond de Goncourt recorded in his diary that Degas spoke of the 'delicate muddiness of Velazquez' and the 'silhouettishness of Mantegna', contrary qualities which he sought to combine in his own art.

With no need to support himself or to struggle for the 'Prix de Rome', a scholarship which took artists to Rome at the expense of the French state, Degas set off in 1856 for three years' travel in Italy, during which he was able to study the art of the past at first hand. He was later to describe these years as 'the most extraordinary period of my life.' Surviving notebooks from his Italian stay reveal what he looked at and the kind of private feelings which he later kept carefully hidden. The relatively few surviving paintings of the period, such as *Roman Beggar Woman* or the portraits of his grandfather, Hilaire Degas, and the Bellelli family, while hardly 'advanced' in terms of contemporary French painting, show a degree of accomplishment and maturity unexpected in an artist with so little training and experience. In fact they need no apologies. They are masterpieces on their own terms.

In the late 1850s and early 1860s Degas worked on a number of ambitious history pictures, including *Jephthah's Daughter, Semiramis Building Babylon* and *The Misfortunes of the Town of Orléans*. Manet later scathingly remarked that Degas was still painting *Semiramis* when he himself had already turned his attention to modern life. Degas' preoccupation with history painting in these years put him in direct opposition to the cherished aims of the more progressive artists of the period, as did his concern with line and contour. The fact that Degas never renounced his early history pictures, but continued to work on them from time to time and to show them with pride to visitors to his studio, is a reminder of the artificiality of the traditional categorization of nineteenth-century French painting into opposing groups. Degas even considered publicly exhibiting history pictures long after his conversion to modern-life themes. *Young Spartans*, another of his early history paintings, figures in the fifth Impressionist exhibition catalogue of 1880 (although it seems that in fact it was not shown).

No one could have predicted Degas' future identification with Impressionism from this early group of historical pictures. Instead they seem much closer to the proto-Symbolist work of Puvis de Chavannes and Gustave Moreau. It is worthwhile at this point looking in more detail at Degas' relationship with these two maverick artists who were in revolt against the materialism of the mid-nineteenth century and against everything associated with the term 'modern life'. At a time when Manet was responding to Baudelaire's call to find the beauty in contemporary, everyday life, the escape of Puvis de Chavannes and Moreau into an imaginary world of ideal beauty struck 'progressive' critics as eccentric and anachronistic. At the same time their rejection of the slick formulae of academic history painting and their creation of personal and highly original styles upset the more conservative critics. It was not until the rise of the Symbolist movement in the 1880s that they began to look 'modern'.

Degas came to know Moreau when both were living in Rome at the end of 1857. The cultured and charming Moreau, who was eight years older than Degas, soon established an influential position amongst Degas' circle of young artist friends. During the year 1858, Degas came completely under Moreau's spell and the two artists established an intense and intimate friendship, spending the months of June to August together in Florence. After Moreau left to join his parents in Milan, Degas repeatedly wrote to urge his return in terms which show his dependence upon the older artist: 'I am really sending this to you to help me wait for your return more patiently, whilst hoping for a letter from you . . . How I miss the encouragement you used to give me . . . I do hope you will not put off your return; you left more than a month ago and you promised that you would spend no more than two months in Venice and Milan.'

Moreau encouraged Degas' love of the Renaissance masters and also kindled an enthusiasm for Delacroix that was to last for the rest of Degas' life. The influence of Moreau on Degas' own work is perhaps most visible in *Semiramis Building Babylon*. The subject itself is typical of Moreau, who loved to paint legendary queens and scenes of oriental splendour. The fantastic city in the background, with its strange technique of what look like stencilled lines and loosely applied patches of colour, is strongly reminiscent of many similar scenes in the backgrounds of Moreau's paintings. Although Moreau kept a portrait which Degas painted of him until the end of his life, the two artists drifted apart in later years and Moreau's art became the victim of some of Degas' more caustic witticisms.

Degas was never on such intimate terms with Puvis de Chavannes, but the two artists knew and admired each other throughout their long careers. They came from similar social backgrounds (something which was important to Degas) and in the years around 1870 would have met frequently at the home of the Morisots, where both carried on a mildly flirtatious friendship with the Impressionist painter Berthe Morisot. The behaviour of Puvis de Chavannes was, in fact, more than flirtatious and there is reason to believe that he was on intimate terms with Morisot. According to Degas' early biographer, Lemoisne, a nude by Puvis de Chavannes hung in Degas' bedroom until the end of his life. In the 1890s, Degas wrote to the sculptor Bartholomé about the beautiful singer, Rose Caron, 'Divine Mme Caron; when I spoke to her I compared her to the figures of Puvis de Chavannes.' On another occasion Degas said of him, 'Nobody has equalled him in finding the right place for the figures in a composition. Try to displace one of his figures by a point or a line, you will not be able to; it's impossible.' This was surely the greatest possible compliment from an artist who was himself so fastidious in the placing of figures.

The frieze-like disposition of figures and their statuesque attitudes in *Semiramis* and *Young Spartans* bears a striking resemblance to the work of Puvis de Chavannes. Both artists succeeded in creating a style which was classical and timeless without being clichéd or academic. As Puvis was himself only just developing his mature style in the 1860s it is not clear which artist was influencing the other or if it was simply a case of parallel development.

Lemoisne tells us that Puvis de Chavannes congratulated Degas warmly when he exhibited the last of his history paintings at the Salon of 1865. This was entitled *Scenes of Warfare in the Middle Ages*, although it has since become known as *The Misfortunes of the Town of Orléans*. Degas' picture may owe a debt to Puvis de Chavannes' treatment of a similar subject, *Bellum*, exhibited four years earlier, although Degas' highly unusual composition (perhaps the result of later alteration or cutting) makes Puvis de Chavannes' picture seem rather staid and conventional in comparison. Degas' puzzling and disturbing picture is the only one of his paintings to depict explicit violence. Scenes of violence towards women were of course not new in Western art (*The Rape of the Sabines* was one of the most popular subjects among the old masters), but they had certainly become more common and more explicit since the advent of Romanticism earlier in the century. Degas would have been well aware of Delacroix's *Death of Sardanapalus*, in which the female victims fall into the most voluptuous poses as they die.

Scenes of rape and violence were immensely popular at the Salon, usually served up under some historical title such as *The Last Days of Babylon, The Fall of Troy, After the Victory of the Moors* or *Norman Pirates of the Ninth Century*. After the Franco-Prussian War such scenes could be given an added patriotic or anti-German slant with titles such as *The Pillage of a Gallo-Roman Dwelling by the Huns*.

Although Degas' picture would seem to fall into a well-established Salon genre, it differs from those of such popular Salon masters as Gérôme, Meissonier or Rochegrosse in that Degas pays no attention to the historical accuracy of the costume and other details. The depiction of archers on horseback is a particularly glaring anachronism. Degas' picture has other, more personal and interesting layers of meaning than the violent fantasies of the Salon artists. It has been plausibly suggested that the picture is a metaphorical criticism of the harsh treatment meted out to the women of New Orleans in the American Civil War by the Unionist troops, who seized the city in 1862 and who were still in much resented occupation when the picture was painted.

The traditional title of the picture, *The Misfortunes of the Town of Orléans*, may have arisen out of a misunderstanding of Degas' intention to make disguised reference to the situation in New Orleans, as there is no comparable recorded incident in the history of the French town of Orléans.

The theme of tension or hostility between the sexes clearly preoccupied Degas in the 1860s, although he treated it more obliquely in his early modern-life pictures such as *Sulking* and *Interior* and most subtly in his portraits, such as that of the Bellelli family.

Degas' conversion to the use of subject matter taken from modern life did not happen suddenly, but evolved in the late 1860s through a series of pictures which are hard to classify. Perhaps the strangest of these is the portrait of

Mlle Fiocre in the ballet *La Source* entitled, *Mlle Fiocre; à propos du ballet de 'La Source'*. This picture, which Degas exhibited at the Salon of 1868, is a mixture of portrait (it is Degas' only recognisable depiction of a famous dancer apart from the long-retired Jules Perrot), ballet scene, history picture and orientalist fantasy. Like so many of his later ballet scenes, it seems to show a moment of rest during a rehearsal rather than the performance of the ballet itself. Unlike the later pictures, there is no sense of a scene taking place on stage. The rocks and the pool seem to be real rather than stage props.

Another key transitional work is *The Orchestra of the Opera*, the first in a series of pictures of orchestra pits. The picture is a highly original group portrait which includes elements of genre or real life and, at the top of the painting, a small slice of that magical and artificial on-stage world which was to fascinate Degas for the rest of his life. With each picture in this series, the stage gradually becomes larger, until the orchestra pit disappears altogether, leaving only the silhouetted tops of the musical instruments which appear in so many pictures of the 1870s.

Degas was relatively slow to answer the call which writers such as Champfleury, Baudelaire and Duranty had been making since the 1840s, for artists to abandon the painting of 'the frivolous knick-knacks of the past' and to paint what they could see around them. As early as 1845, the poet Baudelaire wrote in a Salon review, 'The true painter of the future will be he who wrests from the contemporary scene its epic side, and shows us how great and poetic we are in our cravats and patent-leather boots.' The most famous and influential expression of this demand came in 1863, with the publication of Baudelaire's essay *The Painter of Modern Life*. Ostensibly a tribute to the illustrator Constantin Guys, it became a virtual manifesto of the ideas which were to direct the art of Manet and Degas. Baudelaire believed it was nothing more than laziness for artists to clothe the figures which they painted in the costume and attitudes of the past. He believed that 'Every period has its own carriage, look and gesture', and that art must capture this if it is to retain its interest for future generations. It was not only Baudelaire's espousal of modernity that was of importance to Degas and Manet, but also his concept of the image and the role of the artist. The artist should not hide himself in an ivory tower, but should be a 'man of the world' and a 'man of the crowd' who looks at the world about him with the freshness and curiosity of a child. At the same time, his elitist ideas of the artist as a dandy whose elegance is a 'symbol of the aristocratic superiority of his spirit', would have struck a profound chord in Degas. Manet's picture *Music in the Tuileries Gardens*, painted in 1862, when he was on terms of close friendship with Baudelaire, is virtually a demonstration of the poet's ideas. Manet shows himself as a top-hatted dandy mixing with an elegant crowd. In some ways, however, Degas expressed Baudelaire's theories in a more complete fashion than Manet did. Degas would certainly have concurred with Baudelaire's assertion that 'all good and true draughtsmen draw from the image inscribed in their brain and not from nature,' and with the poet's cynical and disillusioned view of 'natural man' and his belief that all that is beautiful and noble is the result of reason and calculation. Baudelaire died too early to see his ideas come to fruition in Degas' art of the 1870s.

Baudelaire believed that the attitude of the new painter of modern life to his subject matter would approach that of a novelist. There are certainly intriguing parallels between some of Degas' modern-life subjects and the novels of 'Naturalist' writers such as Zola, Duranty and Edmond de Goncourt, both in the subject matter (the low life of the city, prostitutes, laundresses, or acrobats) and

in their stance of quasi-journalistic accuracy and detachment. Edmond de Goncourt remarked maliciously in his journal on the 'spontaneous understanding between those two evil minds', Degas and Zola, but the two artists were equally malicious about each other. Even at the time of his greatest support for the Impressionists, Zola wrote some spiteful and unsympathetic reviews of Degas' work. Degas found Zola's documentary realism excessive, remarking, 'He gives me the impression of a giant studying a telephone book.' This mutual hostility arose in part, no doubt, from a sense of rivalry. Certainly many of Degas' paintings could have been used as illustrations to scenes in Zola's novels and many of Zola's descriptions (such as the back-stage scenes in *Nana*) might have been inspired by Degas. Whilst the similarities are frequently coincidental and derive from common interests and cultural background, at least one major work by Degas can be directly linked to a novel by Zola: the powerful and disturbing *Interior*, painted in the late 1860s, corresponds in numerous details to a passage in the recently published novel, *Thérèse Raquin*, in which Zola describes the fateful, guilt-ridden wedding night of Thérèse and her lover Laurent.

A writer who built up a close relationship with Degas was the novelist Edmond Duranty, whose ideas came to reflect those of Degas so closely that Degas was suspected of having helped him with his assessment of the Impressionist movement in his pamphlet *The New Painting*, published in 1876.

There was a still greater affinity between Degas and the novelist and diarist Edmond de Goncourt, as the latter immediately sensed when he first visited Degas in 1874. The diary entry of 13 February, in which Goncourt describes the visit, is remarkably astute:

Yesterday I spent the afternoon in the studio of a

painter named Degas. After many attempts, many bearings taken in every direction, he has fallen in love with the modern and, in the modern, he has cast his choice upon laundresses and dancers . . . Degas places before our eyes laundresses and more laundresses, while . . . explaining to us technically the downward pressing and the circular strokes of the iron, etc. etc. Next dancers file by. We are in the foyer of the dancing school where, against the light of a window, fantastically silhouetted dancers' legs are coming down a little staircase, with a brilliant spot of red in a tartan in the midst of all those white, ballooning clouds . . .

The painter shows you his pictures, from time to time adding to his explanations by mimicking a choreographic development, or by imitating, in the language of the dancers, one of their arabesques – and it is really very amusing to see him, with his arms curved, mixing the aesthetics of the dancing master with those of the artist . . . What an original fellow, this Degas – sickly, hypochondriac, with such delicate eyes that he fears losing his sight, and for this very reason he is especially sensitive and aware of the reverse character of things. He is the man . . . who has, in reproducing modern life, best captured its soul.

Edmond de Goncourt insinuated that Degas had taken the idea of using laundresses in the painting from his novel *Manette Salomon*, published in 1867. However, a more likely source of inspiration is the art of Honoré Daumier, who had frequently depicted laundresses. The influences in Degas' turn to modern-life subjects were visual as well as literary, and came from artists of the previous generation, such as Courbet and Daumier, as well as contemporary artists such as Manet and Whistler.

Courbet was the most radical and controversial figure in French art of the 1850s and no progressive French

Daumier, *The Orchestra During the Performance of a Tragedy*, 1852. Metropolitan Museum of Art, New York.

artist of Degas' generation could entirely escape his influence. For Degas, however, the influence of Daumier was more profound and long-lasting. He was a passionate collector of Daumier's work, owning by the end of his life six paintings or drawings and 1,800 lithographs by the great caricaturist. The use of strong contre-jour effects to create expressive silhouettes and the unusually heavy and volumetric treatment of the human form in Degas' depiction of laundresses in his paintings of around 1880 show that he had made careful study of Daumier's paintings of the same subject which had been shown at the first major retrospective exhibition of his work in 1879. However, Degas' interest in Daumier's lithographs goes back well before this to the point in the late 1860s when he began to explore a similar range of subject matter. Theodore Reff has demonstrated how Degas borrowed not only a wide range of subjects from Daumier (laundresses, café-concerts, art-collectors) but some of his more radical compositional devices such as the use of unusual viewpoints and the cutting of figures. Degas' originality here, as with his borrowings from Japanese woodcut prints, lay in his transformation of elements from art forms then regarded as popular and ephemeral into 'high art'.

Amongst the great artists of his own generation, the one with whom Degas had most in common was undoubtedly Edouard Manet. In addition to being five or six years older than most of the other members of the Impressionist circle, they also came from a somewhat more elevated social background, which meant that they not only met in artists' cafés such as the Guerbois and the Nouvelle Athènes but also in the houses of each other's parents and numerous common friends.

Both Manet and Degas cherished a deep love of the old masters. They were said to have first met while copying in the Louvre. They admired the Venetians, Velazquez and Delacroix, but Manet was less enthusiastic than Degas about such essentially linear artists as Mantegna, Holbein and Ingres. For all their common interests, Manet and Degas represented the long-standing dichotomy in Western art between the 'linear' and the 'painterly'. This is not to say that Manet was not capable of powerfully expressive contour, nor Degas of exquisite colour, but the chief beauty of Manet's art lies perhaps in his sensuous and visceral use of paint, whereas Degas thought essentially in terms of line and often seems to draw with the brush. Degas disliked the glutinous properties of oil as a medium; he rarely used an impasto, preferring a matt and even surface.

In the 1860s Manet was undoubtedly the stronger and more dominant artist of the two. Though only a year older, his talent matured earlier than that of Degas and he turned towards the use of modern urban subject matter several years earlier than Degas. In the 1870s, the balance between the two artists changed. Manet's painting *The Waitress* in the National Gallery, London, shows the clear influence of Degas' compositional methods, whilst retaining Manet's characteristic and exciting use of paint. Despite the barbed comments which frequently passed between the two artists and a serious quarrel occasioned by Manet's mutilation of a painting by Degas, Degas never lost his respect for Manet's work, which he continued to collect eagerly after Manet's premature death in 1883.

Two other important influences on Degas in his early maturity were those of contemporary English art and Japanese woodcut prints. His interest in English painting was probably triggered by the English section at the Paris Exhibition of 1867, which made an impression on several French painters and critics. He wrote down the titles of several of the English exhibits in his notebooks. Over the next few years, one remarks interesting parallels between Degas' work and that of his English contemporaries, particularly in his concern with modern genre painting, with narrative and with the depiction of psychological tension between male and female figures in such pictures as *Sulking* and *Interior*. Degas' chief source of information about the contemporary English art scene was most probably his friend James McNeill Whistler, who was the most important channel of Anglo-French influences in both directions in these years, and James Tissot, who fled to London in 1871 after the Paris Commune, in which he

Rossetti, Study of a Woman's Head for *Found*, c1853–57.
Birmingham Museum and Art Gallery.

had been implicated. Degas' letters to Tissot show that for a short time in the early 1870s, he cherished the ambition of establishing his reputation and fortune in England. The only major Victorian painter mentioned by name in these letters was Millais, whose *Eve of St. Agnes* Degas would have seen in the 1867 exhibition and which may have influenced his treatment of the shadowy recesses of his own *Interior*. The 1869 painting *Melancholy*, which is so exceptional in Degas' work for its mood of heavy pathos and in the languorous Pre-Raphaelite beauty of the subject, raises the possibility that Degas may have gained some knowledge of the work of Dante Gabriel Rossetti, possibly through Whistler, who was on friendly terms with both artists.

After the forcible opening up of Japan to Western trade in 1853 by the American Commander Perry, Japanese objects flooded into the West and started a craze 'for all one sees that's Japanese' (in the words of W.S. Gilbert in his satirical libretto for the operetta *Patience*). In particular, Japanese woodcut prints proved a revelation to Western artists. At a time when the underlying principles of Western art were being questioned, Japanese woodcuts seemed to provide many of the answers. For a period of fifty years, virtually every avant-garde French painter (Cézanne being the only major exception) was influenced to a greater or lesser extent and in a surprising variety of ways by Japanese woodcuts. Degas was not the first French artist to see the possibilities of Japanese prints; his friend, Félix Braquemond, is usually credited with that. More significantly, from the early 1860s Manet's work shows the clear influence of Japanese prints in the flattening of forms and the use of firm, bounding contours. However, it is arguable that of all the many European artists affected by the discovery of Japanese art, Degas made the most original and creative use of this influence. Unlike Manet's *Woman with the Fans*, Monet's *La Japonaise*, Whistler's *The Princess from the Land of Porcelain* or Renoir's *Portrait of Mme. Charpentier*, Degas' paintings almost never show traces of *japonaiserie* (the use of Japanese accessories for exotic effect). Instead, he was far more interested in the underlying principles of Japanese art (*japonisme*), particularly in composition and the rendering of space. The earliest example of *japonisme* in Degas' art may be seen perhaps in the asymmetrical and unconventional composition of *Woman with the Chrysanthemums*, painted in 1865. The empty space at the centre of *The Misfortunes of the Town of Orléans* and the cutting of the figures on the right also look strikingly Japanese, although these effects may have been accentuated by later alterations. It was not until the 1870s that

Degas experimented more adventurously with stylistic features associated with Japanese art: asymmetry, high viewpoints, flattening of space, startling juxtapositions of near and far and the cutting of figures by the edge of the canvas or by architectural features. Degas was less attracted than Manet by the flat areas of bright colour and shadowless forms also characteristic of Japanese art, although these too can be seen in pictures such as the 1876–77 *On the Beach* and the portrait of Carlo Pellegrini.

Curiously, most of these features of Degas' art of the 1870s may also be attributed to the influence of photography. Although Japanese prints look very different from photographs and later encouraged artists such as Gauguin and Van Gogh to break with the naturalistic depiction of the world in favour of a flat, stylized technique, photography and Japanese prints were, for a time, mutually reinforcing influences. Both brought home to artists the artificiality of traditional Western linear perspective and centralized composition and the way that Western painters had uniformly modelled forms to give a sense of sculptural volume.

Like several other nineteenth-century French artists, Degas painted pictures in the shape of Japanese fans, although even with these, he seems to have made a point of avoiding obviously exotic subject matter. Although he had no interest in exoticism, he nevertheless showed a strong affinity for the range of subject matter favoured by Japanese artists: the theatre, brothels and various other urban entertainments. However, in the final analysis, it is hard to pin down the extent and significance of the Japanese influence on Degas' work: it may be that it merely confirmed the direction in which he would have travelled in any case.

The tragic events of 1870–71 – the Franco-Prussian War and the Paris Commune – followed by Degas' lengthy visit to his American relatives from late 1872 to early 1873, mark a hiatus and a turning point in his career. In the years up to 1870, Degas had absorbed a wide range of influences. He had already painted a number of masterpieces, and he had finally turned to the depiction of subject matter taken from modern life. In particular, he had begun to tackle the two subjects with

Hiroshige, *Ferry at Haneda*, c1858, woodcut print from *One Hundred Views of Edo*. Reproduced by courtesy of the Trustees of the British Museum, London.

Yoshitoshi, *A Poem by Abe No Nakamara*, from the series *One Hundred Aspects of the Moon*, 1888. Author's collection.

which he would later be most associated, the ballet and the racecourse, in pictures which already show an experimental approach to composition. However, it was not until after Degas' return from New Orleans in 1873 that the mature artist emerged and embarked upon the two most productive decades of his career.

At the outbreak of war, Degas joined the National Guard, along with Manet and several other artists. Berthe Morisot's mother gently mocked their bellicose attitudes: 'He (Degas) and Manet nearly came to blows arguing over the methods of defence and the use of the National Guard, although each of them was ready to die to save the country . . . M. Degas has joined the artillery, and by his own account has not yet heard a cannon go off.' Degas' reaction to the Paris Commune was not that of the die-hard reactionary he was later to become. He did not allow Tissot's involvement with the Commune to interfere with their friendship, and Mme Morisot expressed surprised indignation that Degas was not in favour of the bloody repression of the communards.

Degas spent five months in New Orleans, staying with his brothers, who worked there as cotton merchants. His letters to France reveal the closeness of his family ties and a warm and affectionate side of his character which is at variance with his usual image as sharp-tongued and misanthropic. Degas was so taken by the family life of his brothers that he even briefly contemplated having a family of his own.

He wrote to Tissot: 'A good family; it is a really good thing to be married, to have good children, to be free of the need of being gallant. Ye gods, it is really time one thought about it.'

Degas was delighted by the richly exotic local colour. He wrote back glowingly of the 'negresses of all shades, holding in their arms little white babies, so white, against white houses with columns of fluted wood and in gardens of orange trees, and the ladies in muslin against the fronts of their little houses, and the steamboats with two chimneys as tall as factory chimneys . . .' Unlike Gauguin fifteen years later in Martinique, Degas made no attempt to paint any of this. He offered various excuses – that the light was too strong for his weak eyes, that the climate

Degas, *Danseuses*, c.1879. Photo: Archives Durand Ruel, Paris.

induced laziness. The real reason seems to have been that he was not happy with painting anything that was not thoroughly familiar to him. 'It is not good to make Parisian and Louisiana art indiscriminately, it is liable to turn into the *Monde Illustré*. And then nothing but a really long stay can reveal the customs of a people, that is to say their charm – instantaneousness is photography, nothing more . . . '

When Degas returned to France in 1873, he found a very different cultural atmosphere from that of the relaxed and hedonistic final years of the Second Empire, which had been swept away by the Franco-Prussian War.

The conservative bourgeoisie, which was now firmly in control of the government and the art establishment, had been thoroughly frightened by the excesses of the Paris Commune and the spectre of revolution. The mood of France in the early 1870s might be compared to that of America in the McCarthyist period. Any deviation from accepted norms was regarded with deep suspicion as potentially subversive. The new republic was in many ways more repressive than the relatively benign dictatorship of Louis Napoléon, particularly in matters of artistic tolerance.

Degas had been intensely dissatisfied with the Salon even before the war. In 1870, he had published an open letter to the Salon jury, listing his grievances and exhorting, 'Gentlemen, you must know that we expect a lot from you; above all, a lot of innovations.' Needless to say, in the intensely conservative post-war mood, the innovations were not forthcoming. Renoir found his works rejected by the Salon in 1872 and 1873 and other progressive artists, such as Monet, Sisley, Pissarro and Degas, did not even bother to submit their work. A special exhibition of refused works was held in 1873 (repeating the notorious Salon des Refusés of ten years earlier), but this provided no long-term solution to the intransigence of the Salon jury and to the disadvantages of such a vast exhibition which, as Degas pointed out in his open letter, seemed to have little to do with art.

Towards the end of 1873, when Monet mooted the idea of an independent group exhibition, Degas responded enthusiastically and urged his friends to join in too (unsuccessfully in the case of Manet, Tissot and Legros). It is hard to comprehend the stranglehold which the Salon and its jury had on the Paris art scene in the nineteenth century and the courage required for artists to break with it. With hindsight, the first Impressionist exhibition of 1874 seems to have been one of the great milestones in the history of Western art. At the time it was far from a success, either financial or critical. Indeed, the philistine savagery of the critical response to the Impressionist exhibitions has become legendary. Degas took part in seven of the eight Impressionist shows (more than any major artist except Pissarro and Morisot).

When he and the various friends and followers whom he invited to exhibit in the Impressionist shows eventually became a separate faction very much at odds with the landscapists, tensions between the two factions reached a head with the exclusion of Degas and his friends from the seventh Impressionist exhibition in 1882.

The term Impressionist is frequently used so loosely and in such a confusing way that it is necessary at this point to try to define what Impressionism was and what, if anything, Degas had in common with it. Impressionism was principally concerned with landscape and with the truthful recording of effects of light and atmosphere. The Impressionist 'method' (if one can use this word for such an instinctive and empirical kind of art) involved working out of doors, directly from nature, and required the abandonment of the concept of 'finish'. Traditional draughtsmanship – the contouring of forms – was also sacrificed in favour of rendering light and atmosphere with small broken touches of colour.

Landscape plays a very minor role in Degas' art and he reserved his most cutting witticisms for artists who felt it necessary to work out of doors. He told Vollard, 'You know what I think of people who work out in the open. If I were the government, I would have a special brigade of gendarmes to keep an eye on artists who paint landscapes from nature. Oh, I don't mean to kill anyone; just a little dose of bird-shot now and then as a warning.' Degas was most opposed to Impressionism in his insistence that drawing and contour were the very basis of his art. What Degas shared with the Impressionists was his opposition to the art establishment and the kind of anaemic art exhibited at the Salon. Like the Impressionists he flouted traditional expectations of 'finish' and like them he was committed to painting modern life and the real world in a detached and truthful fashion, (although Degas' 'modern life' was urban, whereas that of the Impressionists was principally suburban).

Both Degas and the Impressionists rejected the kind of narrative found in academic Salon paintings. (There are important narrative elements in some of Degas' paintings such as *Sulking* and *Absinthe*, but presented in a far more subtle way). Instead, the Impressionists aimed to present a small slice of reality apparently perceived in a moment. This momentary character is created by their rapid and

Degas, *Rehearsal of a Ballet on Stage*, 1874. Musée d'Orsay, Paris.

spontaneous technique and reinforced by such elements as blurred moving figures in townscapes or steam trains hurtling through the backgrounds of landscapes. The momentary in Degas' work is created by means of compositions carefully constructed to look casual or accidental with figures wandering in or out of view, cut by the picture edge. Degas always maintained that, despite the momentary character of his images, there was nothing spontaneous in his art and he would never have wished to paint (in the words of Monet), 'as the bird sings'.

Finally, it must be said that Degas did not regard himself as an Impressionist and deeply resented being regarded as part of an Impressionist 'school'. Of all the painters of the Impressionist circle, Degas was probably least in sympathy with Monet – the arch-Impressionist and the artist for whom the term was first coined. It is significant that Degas' collection, which contained works by Pissarro, Morisot and Sisley and by the Post-Impressionists Cézanne, Van Gogh and Gauguin, contained nothing by Monet. Pissarro reported Degas' comment that Monet's art was that of a 'skilful but not profound decorator.' When Degas met Monet in front of some of the latter's pictures at Durand-Ruel's gallery, he burst out tactlessly, 'Let me get out of here! Those reflections in the water hurt my eyes!' later adding the comment, 'His pictures always were too draughty for me!

Béraud, *Backstage at the Opera*, 1889. Musée Carnavalet, Paris.

Degas, *Two Dancers on the Stage*, 1874. Courtauld Institute Galleries, London: Courtauld Collection.

If it had been any worse, I should have had to turn up my coat collar.'

It was in the 1870s that Degas became known as 'the painter of dancers' and even today it is dancers that are most likely to come to mind at the mention of his name. Approximately half of his entire output depicts ballet dancers. This fact seems all the more remarkable when one remembers that he did not turn to the ballet for inspiration until 1867, when he painted *Mlle. Fiocre: à propos du ballet de 'La Source'* and that he did not take up the theme with any regularity until 1873, when he was nearly 40.

The reasons for Degas' preoccupation with the ballet are complex and various. Firstly, he had a genuine passion for music. In 1872 he wrote to a friend from New Orleans, 'I need music so much – there is no opera here this winter. Yesterday evening I went to a rather monotonous concert . . .'; and a few days later he complained in a letter to Henri Rouart, 'The lack of an opera is a real privation.' Back in Paris, Degas was a regular opera- and concert-goer until late in life and Vollard recalled how he would always hum 'some old tune' while he worked.

Degas numbered at least two distinguished composers amongst his friends – Emmanuel Chabrier, who wrote the ever popular *España* and the delightful and witty comic opera *Le Roi Malgré Lui* and Ernest Reyer, who sought to outdo Wagner with his operatic setting of the Nibelungen legends entitled *Sigurd*. What Degas thought of Reyer's over-inflated efforts may be deduced from a page in a notebook of 1858 on which Degas imitated the signatures of various famous men. Degas' version of Reyer's signature ends with a hilariously ribald phallic flourish.

The exciting visual possibilities presented by the interior of an opera house undoubtedly helped to kindle Degas' interest in the ballet: unusual viewpoints from an opera box, or from the orchestra pit up to the stage, startling juxtapositions of near and far, light and dark, illusion and reality, beauty and banality. Degas was as fascinated by artificial theatrical light as the Impressionists were by sunlight, as is shown by the detailed notes that he made before painting the ballet scene from *Robert the Devil* in 1872:

Shadow carried from the score onto the rounded back of the rostrum – dark grey background – bowstring brightly lit by the lamps, head of Georges in silhouette, light red shadows – flesh tones.

In the receding arches the moonlight barely licks the columns – on the ground the effect pinker and warmer than I made it – black vault, the beams indistinct . . .

The theatre boxes a mass of dark lacquered brick red – in the director's box, light-red, pink face, striking shirts, vivid black . . . '

One can be fairly sure that an interest in classical dance for its own sake was not a determining factor in Degas' numerous depictions of dancers. It is a strange fact that

Degas, *The Curtain*, c1880. Collection of Mr and Mrs Paul Mellon, Upperville, Virginia.

when Degas was making his celebrated images of dancers, ballet in France was at its lowest ebb both artistically and morally. It was not until 1909, when Diaghilev brought the Ballets Russes to Paris, that ballet was revived there as a serious art form and by this time Degas was almost blind. The only dancer of distinction that Degas painted, apart from Mlle Fiocre, was the aged Jules Perrot, long after his dancing days were over. The writer Edmond de Goncourt noted in his diary, after visiting Degas in his studio in 1874, that the artist was able to demonstrate various balletic positions (the sight of the staid and middle-aged Degas making pirouettes must have been extraordinary!), although most of Degas' dancers seem curiously graceless and are hardly good examples of classical dancing technique. More often than not they are shown rehearsing, resting, scratching, yawning, but rarely in actual performance. Whenever Degas did paint a performance he always made sure that some element of banal reality intruded – the arm of a female spectator holding a fan or a pair of opera glasses, the legs of a dark-suited gentleman standing in the wings or the top of a musical instrument rising from the orchestra pit.

What interested Degas much more than the actual performance was the somewhat dubious atmosphere backstage. Nowadays it is hard to imagine just how louche the reputation of the ballet was in Degas' time. It was quite accepted that many of the young working-class girls who formed the corps de ballet would supplement their meagre income with prostitution and that the mothers who hovered around them would sometimes act as go-betweens rather than as chaperones. For men about town it was a matter of status to have a mistress in the ballet, and backstage areas of the opera swarmed with predatory, top-hatted men (access backstage was a sought-after privilege and there are several surviving letters from Degas to various influential friends begging this favour).

It was expected that every opera should have a balletic interlude in the second act so that members of the fashionable Jockey Club could arrive late after a leisurely dinner and see their mistresses on stage. When Wagner refused to accommodate their wishes at the Paris pre-mière of his opera *Tannhäuser* in 1861, the members of the Jockey Club disrupted the performance, causing the most notorious operatic fiasco of the century.

It was probably Degas' childhood friend Ludovic Halévy who introduced the artist to this shady backstage milieu. Today, Halévy is chiefly remembered for the witty libretti which he and Henri Meilhac supplied for Offen-bach's operettas. They also co-wrote the libretto for Bizet's *Carmen*, the first opera to introduce as characters on the operatic stage the kind of working-class girls that fascinated Degas. In 1870, Halévy published the first in a series of novels about the Cardinal family, two young dancers at the opera, Pauline and Virginie Cardinal, and their unscrupulous parents, M. and Mme. Cardinal, who watch over the young girls' dancing and amorous careers. Degas made a number of mordantly witty monotype illustrations to Halévy's novels.

Degas' oils and pastels, too, are permeated by this equivocal atmosphere, although in his exhibited works he did not make the backstage traffic in flesh quite so explicit. That was left to Degas' less subtle imitators, such as Forain and Béraud.

There is no record of Degas himself taking a mistress among the dancers, but he was clearly attracted to them. Ludovic Halévy's son, Daniel, noted that Degas 'finds them all charming, makes excuses for anything they do, and laughs at everything they say', conjuring up a rather incongruous picture of the normally terse and bad-tempered artist.

After ballet, the subject that Degas turned to most often over his long career was horse-racing. It has been calculated that he produced at least 45 paintings, 20 pastels, around 250 drawings and 17 sculptures on this theme.

It is highly unlikely that Degas ever sat on a horse, at least during the years when he painted them or regularly attended race meetings. The racing pictures, like those of the ballet, were painted in his studio, largely from memory. In the late 1860s he built up an extensive repertoire of figures and poses which were used again and again in endless variations, so ingenious and complex that it is easy not to notice that they have been used before. He supplemented these observations from life with borrow-ings from English sporting prints, photographs and, on one occasion, from a painting by the academic master Ernest Meissonier. In the 1880s, Degas made extensive use of the famous photographs of horses in motion published by the American photographer, Eadweard Muybridge.

Horse-racing was a relatively recent activity in France, introduced from England in the course of the nineteenth century. The race-track at Longchamp in the Bois de Boulogne on the outskirts of Paris, which provided inspiration for Manet and Degas and later for Toulouse Lautrec, was opened in 1857 as part of Baron Haussmann's scheme for urban renewal. The exclusive Jockey Club was founded in 1833. Degas would have seen many of the same people both on the race-track and backstage at the opera. In France even more than in England, horse-breeding and racing became a focus for snobbery and social activities. Of the artists in the Impressionist circle, only Manet and Degas could aspire to the social level of the kind of people involved in horse-breeding and racing and it is significant that none of the other Impressionist artists attempted to paint the subject.

Degas was less interested in the social spectacle of the race-course than Manet (depicted by Degas as a smartly dressed spectator in a drawing of the early 1870s). It is only in pictures of the late 1860s and early 1870s that Degas shows spectators at all and even in these it is often hard to determine where the race is taking place, as Degas takes considerable liberties with topographical accuracy. After the mid-1870s, Degas concentrated on the jockeys themselves and their horses, with usually no more than a minimal landscape background. His view of the racing world is quite as partial and exclusive as his view of the ballet. Just as he preferred to show a rehearsal rather than an actual performance, he also chose to paint the moment before a race rather than the race itself (only two of his pictures show a race actually taking place).

Although the compositions were carefully constructed in the studio with an almost abstract sense of design taking precedence over descriptive information, Degas also sought to give the impression that what we see is a little fragment of reality, captured as though by a snapshot. Figures overlap and are cut by the edge of the picture as they wander casually in and out of view. In the later racing pictures we almost never see the complete figure of a horse.

It is instructive to compare a characteristic race-course scene of Degas' maturity, such as *At the Races, Gentlemen Jockeys*, with the most famous nineteenth-century English painting of the subject, William Powell Frith's *Derby Day*, exhibited at the Royal Academy in 1858. In the sense that both artists desire to present us with an apparent fragment of reality, both might be termed 'realist', but the comparison only serves to underline what extremely varied interpretations may be given to the term 'realist' – even within the context of mid-nineteenth-century European painting. Frith's idea of painting reality is to give us as much descriptive information as he can possibly cram into one picture. If we so wish, we can count the number of buttons on a jacket or see the individual hairs on a child's head. Degas' carriage vanishes out of the right-hand side of his picture, offering us no more than a tantalizing glimpse of the elegant hats and coiffures of the ladies occupying it. Frith not only gives us every detail of the appearance of the people in the carriage in his picture, but even indicates their moral character. It would be easy enough to write their entire life-story, as English critics were sometimes inclined to do in the lengthy reviews that they devoted to such pictures.

Compared to the epigrammatic clarity and economy of Degas' composition, Frith's seems like a great, sprawling Dickens' novel, teeming with characters, plots, sub-plots and humorous, moralizing and sentimental asides. Degas, who always maintained a stance of fastidious reserve and detachment in his art, would have shrunk from Frith's sermonizing on the evils of gambling and his sentimental

Powell Frith, *Derby Day*, 1856–58. The Tate Gallery, London.

anecdotalism.

Lastly, it is fascinating to compare the use made by the two artists of photography.

Like many Victorian artists, Frith strove to compete with the camera's ability to record detail. Oscar Wilde once unkindly dismissed Frith as the man who had 'raised art to the dignity of photography'. In his memoirs, Frith writes scathingly of photography and its effect upon art, but he was not above hiring a professional photographer to take photographs of the grandstands at Epsom, which he used for the background of *Derby Day*. For Frith, photographs were merely an aid to topographical accuracy, and a welcome short-cut to the kind of detailed finish which his public expected. (Despite the photographs, *Derby Day* still took Frith 'fifteen month incessant labour'

to complete). For progressive French artists, on the contrary, photography obviated the necessity of the painstaking recording of detail by the painter. Like Japanese woodcut prints, photography and, in particular, snapshots showed up the artificiality of traditional European methods of composition and pointed to new ways of perceiving reality and composing pictures. Of all the artists of his generation, Degas understood this best and was able to make the most creative use of photography, confirming the prophetic words which Delacroix had written in his journal in 1853, 'Truly, if a man of genius should use the daguerreotype as it ought to be used, he will raise himself to heights unknown to us.'

There were three other subjects, apart from ballet and the race-course, which inspired extensive series of paintings in the late 1870s and early 1880s – the café-concert, laundresses and milliners. Each of these enabled Degas to explore further his fascination with the working-class Parisienne. Café-concerts were amongst the most popular of Parisian entertainments during the Second Empire and the Third Republic. They first appeared in Paris in the 1830s; mushrooming in numbers after the 1867 Universal Exhibition, they reached a peak of nearly 200 in the early 1880s. The café-concert was something between a beer hall and a concert hall: drinks were served, people moved around and prostitutes sought customers, whilst singers, dancers, acrobats and jugglers performed their acts. Degas clearly revelled in the bustling, socially mixed and somewhat equivocal atmosphere. The café-concert paintings share many visual features with early ballet scenes such as the *Orchestra of the Opera* or *Ballet Scene from 'Robert the Devil'*. There are the same striking divisions between dark orchestra pit, audience and brightly-lit stage; the same magical effect of gas footlights dissolving the solidity of forms on stage (for example, the way in which the outstretched arm of the singer in red in *Aux Ambassadeurs* dissolves into nothing). Once again, the scrolled top of the double-bass rises up out of the orchestra to form a *repoussoir* against the shimmering images on stage. Degas shows a marvellous ability to capture the characteristic pose and gesture of a singer leaning forward to belt out a risqué song or raising a black-gloved hand to emphasize a high note or an outrageous *double entendre*. As at the ballet, Degas concentrated exclusively on the female performers and completely ignored the many popular male performers at the various café-concerts.

Another kind of working-class Parisienne which preoccupied Degas in the 1870s was the prostitute. With two major exceptions, *Absinthe* and *Women on a Café Terrace, Evening*, Degas tended to confine his images of prostitutes to the more private medium of the monotype. When he showed *Women on a Café Terrace, Evening* at the third

Impressionist exhibition in 1877, he was accused of trying to shock. Degas was not alone in this preoccupation. Prostitution was an important subject for painters and novelists on both sides of the channel, and was far more widespread in nineteenth-century Europe than it is today. Economic necessity – the inability of women to support themselves by other means – forced large numbers into various kinds of prostitution. Prostitution was also the reverse side of Victorian prudery in sexual matters. (Paris was somewhat less prudish than other cities, hence the reputation it gained at this time as a kind of 'sin city').

It is highly revealing to compare Degas' most impressive image of a fallen woman, *Absinthe*, with English paintings on similar themes, such as Egg's *Past and Present*, Rossetti's *Found* or Holman-Hunt's *The Awakening Conscience*. It is interesting to note that many English people would have been able to do precisely this, as *Absinthe* was first exhibited in England in 1876. Although the picture figures in the catalogue of the second Impressionist exhibition under the title *In a Café*, it seems that, as on many other occasions, Degas was unable to finish it on time, and instead sold it directly to an English art collector, a Captain Henry Hill, of Brighton. Captain Hill lent it to the Third Annual Winter Exhibition of Modern Pictures at the Brighton Pavilion in 1876. What the good citizens of Victorian Brighton can have made of this provocative picture is hard to imagine.

The most obvious difference between *Absinthe* and a picture like Holman-Hunt's *The Awakening Conscience*, which would have been picked up by Victorian art lovers, is the former's loose finish and lack of attention to detail. Hunt crams his pictures with telling detail. We are expected to notice, for instance, that the woman wears rings on every finger except that reserved for the wedding ring. No doubt hoping to forestall criticisms of its lack of finish, Captain Hunt took the precaution of exhibiting his

Holman-Hunt, *The Awakening Conscience*, 1853. The Tate Gallery, London.

picture under the title *A Sketch in a French Café*. Only the following year Ruskin accused Whistler of 'throwing a pot of paint' in the public's face by exhibiting a loosely-brushed picture which was deemed to be unfinished. The notorious libel trial which resulted from Ruskin's outburst hinged on the vexed question of 'finish'.

Absinthe is, in fact, an exceptionally sketchy work even for Degas at this period. X-ray photographs indicate that the woman's features were once more defined and that

Degas chose to repaint them in a looser and more economical fashion. The newspapers and match container in the foreground, the woman's splayed feet and her water carafe are indicated with the barest minimum of brush strokes. Her torso and shoulders and the marble table tops are crudely contoured in black. The fact that Degas omitted to paint any support for the table tops would also have seemed like unforgivable carelessness to the literal-minded Victorians.

Absinthe seems to have gone unnoticed by art critics when it was shown in Brighton, but when it reached London in the 1890s it caused outrage and controversy. The British critics were shocked, not only by the bold technique, but even more by Degas' treatment of his subject matter. What disturbed them most was the painter's stance of apparent moral neutrality. Unlike Hunt in *The Awakening Conscience*, Degas refused to preach a sermon or to gloat over the woman's predicament. Conversely, one could point out that, unlike many English painters, he shows no sign of social conscience or sympathy for the woman's plight. As though to tell us that the picture is intended as a kind of 'reportage' on contemporary life, Degas signs his name across the newspaper in the foreground.

Degas succeeds in conveying a mood of alienation and loneliness through visual means and without resorting to the story-telling devices of contemporary English painters. He uses a range of drab, dirty, earth colours far removed from the joyous palette of the Impressionists or the gaudy luminosity of *The Awakening Conscience* and thin, rather scrappy application of paint, equally far from the luscious *belle peinture* of Manet.

Perhaps the most remarkable and original aspect of the picture is the composition and the way in which Degas arranges all the elements so as to manipulate the reaction of the viewer, who is apparently seated at the table of which we see part in the foreground. He or she is half-heartedly reading the newspaper on its baton whilst observing the couple on the right of the picture. We are linked to them visually by the newspapers on the left. At the same time, the table tops create a kind a barrier which isolates the woman. The 'body language' of the two figures, her slumped shoulders, inelegantly splayed legs and unfocused facial expression, and his gaze away from her and out of the picture speak of their unhappiness and mutual indifference. It says much of the difference between French and English artists of this period that Hunt was willing to repaint the facial expression of the woman in the *The Awakening Conscience* to please the picture's first owner, who found it too painful. One can well imagine the answer that Captain Hill would have received had he made such a request of Degas.

The monotypes of brothels which Degas produced in the late 1870s make his depiction of prostitution in *Absinthe* and *Women on a Café Terrace, Evening* seem almost tame by comparison. They are marked by a robust humour which is exceptional in Degas' work. The savage boldness of technique and the caricatural exaggerations of these images are tempered by a quality which might be called affectionate. Although some of these monotypes are extremely explicit, there is none of the lubricity which characterizes the endless depictions of the female nude to be found on the walls of the Salon every year in the second half of the nineteenth century. The frankness of Degas' depiction of human sexuality would have been extraordinary in any period of Western art, let alone in the prudish nineteenth century, and possibly owes something to the study of similar subjects in Japanese woodcut prints.

The years around 1880 saw the climax of Degas' interest in portraiture. Whereas the early portraits had mostly been of members of Degas' family, by the late

Degas, *The Serious Client*, c1879. National Gallery of Canada, Ottawa.

1870s Degas tended to choose his subjects from amongst his circle of friends – writers and critics such as Edmond Duranty and Diego Martelli, collectors such as Ernst May and Henri Rouart, and fellow artists such as Mary Cassatt and Henri Michel-Lévy. Degas was never willing to accept portrait commissions from strangers (no doubt his sharp tongue and the equally uncompromising sharpness of his art saved him from the importunate society women from whom Renoir had to defend himself in later years). Degas was less interested in making exact or flattering facial likenesses than in producing a more complete image of a personality through the sitter's pose and his or her everyday surroundings. Edmond Duranty surrounded by his books, and Ernest May conducting his business at the Paris stock exchange, both exhibited at the fourth Impressionist exhibition in 1879, are examples of a kind of painting which combines traditional portraiture with elements of genre painting in a highly original and personal way.

In the 1880s, most of the leading Impressionists went through crises of self-doubt which affected the quality of their work. Degas, however, seemed to go from strength to strength. Pissarro, with whom Degas had many clashes over the organization of the Impressionist exhibitions, wrote to his son Lucien in May 1883 that Degas was 'without doubt the greatest artist of the period.' Renoir too recognized a greatness and timelessness in Degas' art at this time which set him apart from his contemporaries, comparing works by Degas at various times to the Parthenon, Chartres Cathedral and Egyptian bas-reliefs.

Aspects of Degas' art which must have seemed reactionary to some of his Impressionist colleagues in the 1870s, stood him in good stead now that a general reaction had set in to the Impressionist aesthetic. Degas' belief that the example of the old masters could be followed without compromising the artist's modernity, his emphasis on drawing and contour and on working from memory so as to capture the essential and not the ephemeral, his contempt for spontaneity and his much-repeated dictum that a work of art was something artificial, 'apart from nature, which required as much wiliness as the perpetration of a crime', inspired artists who were disillusioned with attempts to work from nature and with the undisciplined formlessness of Impressionism. In letter after letter to his son in the 1880s, Pissarro berates the errors of Impressionism and exhorts him to draw,

'Draw more and more often – remember Degas.' Renoir too turned his back on Impressionism and looked to Ingres, Raphael and Pompeiian frescoes for inspiration. The desire for timelessness and classical qualities in the 1880s is also illustrated by the triumph of Puvis de Chavannes' highly influential mural *The Sacred Wood* in 1884 and in Cézanne's attempts to combine Impressionism with the 'art of the museums'. Seurat too seemed to be attempting to combine Impressionism with classical qualities in painting which his friend Félix Fénéon described as 'modernized Puvis de Chavannes.'

Degas, *Waiting*, second version, 1876–77. Musée Picasso, Paris.

Degas' most remarkable achievement in the 1880s and perhaps of his entire career was in his great series of *toilettes* – women washing and drying themselves and combing their hair. In this series Degas took a radically new approach to the theme of the female nude which has inspired Western artists since the Renaissance. As he told the Irish writer, George Moore, 'Hitherto the nude has always been represented in poses which presuppose an audience, but these women of mine are honest, simple folk, unconcerned by other interests than those involved in their physical condition. Here is another; she is washing her feet. It is as if you looked through the keyhole.'

It could be said that on one level all the great nudes of Western art from Titian to Ingres were pin-ups, showing off their nudity for the delectation of male viewers. This aspect of the female nude began to take precedence over all others in the paintings of Degas' academic contemporaries which, despite their apparent moralizing and prudery and their pretentions to be 'High Art', degenerated to a level close to pornography. Every year the walls of the Salon were covered with hundreds of depictions of the female nude. By the 1890s, it was possible to buy publications containing photogravures of all the most titillating Salon nudes, which were quite simply upmarket dirty magazines. A great deal of ingenuity went into inventing biblical, historical, philosophical or anecdotal titles which would provide the artists with some kind of moral fig-leaf, whilst enabling them to present nudity in the most suggestive ways possible. The salaciousness of these pictures lay not so much in their nudity as in their facial expressions. The allegorical representations of Truth, Beauty, Vice, Progress and Industry, the Venuses, Susannahs and Salomés, all looked out at the top-hatted exhibition-goers with the same enticing and coquettish expressions. It is significant that Degas never shows us the facial features of the women in his *toilettes*. Their faces are either hidden or else blurred beyond recognition. As Degas explained, his subjects were perfectly ordinary women, engaged in perfectly ordinary activities and apparently unaware of being watched. It was precisely the unsexiness of his nudes that most shocked and embarrassed Degas' contemporaries. Even his supporters felt that by stripping the female nude of its sexual allure, he was making an attack upon the female sex. In 1889 the novelist Joris Karl Huysmans wrote an appreciation of Degas' *toilettes* which combines admiration and fascinated disgust:

It seems as though, exasperated by the baseness of his surroundings, he (M. Degas) has resolved to proceed to reprisals and fling in the face of his own century the grossest insult by overthrowing woman, the idol, who has always been so gently treated and whom he degrades by showing her naked in the bath-tub, in the humiliating positions of her private toilet.

And the better to emphasize her origins, he selects a woman who is fat, potbellied, losing, from the plastic viewpoint, all dignity, all grace of line; making her, in fact, regardless of the class to which she may belong, a pork-butcher's wife, a female butcher, in short a creature whose vulgar shape and heavy features suggest her continence and determine her horribleness! . . .

But in addition to this special accent of contempt and hatred, what one should note in these works is the unforgettable truthfulness of the types, caught with a simple, basic style of drawing, with lucid, controlled passion, coldly but feverishly . . . This is no longer the smooth, slippery, eternally naked flesh of goddesses . . . ; this is real, living, unclothed flesh, turned in its ablutions to goose-pimples which will gradually soften away.

Degas, *Woman Drying Herself*, c1889–90. Courtauld Institute
Galleries, London: Courtauld Collection.

Of the people who visited this exhibition, some, confronted by the woman squatting full-face, her belly disclaiming the usual deceptions, would exclaim aloud, indignant at such frankness, yet gripped by the life that emanates from these pastels. They would end by exchanging some shamefaced or disgusted remarks and move away, uttering as their last word: "It's obscene!"

But never was work less obscene, never was work so free from precautionary tricks and ruses, so entirely, decisively chaste. Indeed, it glorifies the disdain of the flesh as no artist has ventured to do since the Middle Ages . . .

No doubt Huysmans exaggerated Degas' perversity for literary effect, just as he had that of Odilon Redon in another famous descriptive passage in his novel *Against Nature*. Neither Degas nor Pissarro had much patience with Huysmans' writings on art. Nevertheless, Degas himself remarked, 'I have perhaps too often considered woman as an animal.' Degas' misogyny was already legendary during his lifetime. Many friends recorded conversations and remarks which showed Degas' hostility to women. In 1869, Berthe Morisot described in a letter to her sister how Degas 'came and sat beside me, pretending to court me, but this courting was confined to a long commentary on Solomon's proverb "Woman is the desolation of the righteous . . ." other characteristic comments are, "What frightens me more than anything else in the world is taking tea in a fashionable tea-room. You would think that you were in a hen-house. Why must women take all that trouble to look so ugly and be so vulgar?" or "Oh! Women can never forgive me; they hate me, they can feel that I am disarming them. I show them without their coquetry, in the state of animals cleaning

Renoir, *Reclining Female Nude*, 1897. Oskar Reinhart Collection, Winterthur, Switzerland.

themselves! . . . They see in me the enemy. Fortunately, for if they did like me, that would be the end of me!"'

Renoir's love of women was as famous as Degas' dislike of them, but Degas' grumpy hostility might be considered less offensive today than Renoir's 'patronizing' love of women. Renoir's remark, 'I can't see myself getting into bed with a lawyer. I like women best when they don't know how to read . . .', is at least as likely to raise hackles as anything said by Degas. The nudes that Renoir was painting in the 1880s and 1890s often make interesting comparisons with those of Degas, but are certainly closer to the traditional male chauvinist pin-up.

Degas would undoubtedly have regarded any discussion of his private life as irrelevant and deeply impertinent. It is inevitable, however, that an artist who devoted most of his life to depicting women and yet seemed not to like them should be the subject of a great deal of speculation. There is in fact remarkably little evidence of any relationship with women, at least of a sexual or strongly emotional nature. Degas apparently kept to the end of his life a portrait drawing of a certain Mlle Volkonska, who had rejected him when he was 19; there has also been speculation about possible relationships with Mary Cassatt and Marie Dihau. As early as 1869, Manet said of Degas to Berthe Morisot, 'He lacks spontaneity; he isn't capable of loving a woman, much less of telling her that he does or doing anything about it.' There has even been speculation fuelled by a joking conversation which Degas had with a model late in life that Degas may have suffered from impotence as the result of venereal disease. When he complained of his weak bladder, the model answered, 'That's what you get for not behaving yourself when you were younger,' to which Degas replied, 'Ah, you minx, remembering all my little secrets . . . '

From time to time the young Degas would express the desire for a wife and family and the older Degas would regret that he was a bachelor. While in Italy in the 1850s he wrote, 'If I can only find a good, simple, tranquil little wife who will understand my cranky humours and with whom I can spend a modest, hard-working life; isn't that a beautiful dream?' It seems, however, that it was no more than a dream and he was speaking more truthfully when he said, 'There is love, and there is work, and we have only one heart.'

Degas' hostile remarks were no doubt self-protective and intended to hide a deep-rooted shyness and insecurity. Vollard says as much: 'It is almost a commonplace that Degas had a peculiar hatred of women. Yet on the other hand, no one loved women as he did; but a kind of shame or modesty, in which there was something like fear, kept him away from them.'

Despite saying that women had no real understanding of art, Degas had the greatest respect for three women artists, Berthe Morisot, Mary Cassatt and Suzanne Valadon, and did everything he could to encourage their work. Berthe Morisot was deeply flattered to be praised for her draughtsmanship by this most exacting of draughtsmen. Cassatt's *Girl Arranging her Hair* occupied a place of honour in Degas' collection and was shown with pride to visitors. Unfortunately, Cassatt destroyed the letters Degas wrote to her, but charming letters exist from him to the 'terrible Maria' as he used to call Suzanne Valadon, begging her to bring 'some wicked and supple drawings.'

From the middle of the 1870s Degas had turned increasingly to pastels and by 1880 he was working more in pastel than in oils. Considering Degas' oft-expressed misogyny there is a certain irony in the fact that the medium with which he became most associated was first successfully exploited by a woman, the Venetian artist Rosalba Carriera, in the early eighteenth century. Following in her footsteps, several mid-eighteenth-century artists, such as Maurice Quentin de La Tour, Liotard and Chardin, raised the medium of pastel to great heights of accomplishment and sophistication. However, by the end of the eighteenth century, pastel had fallen from fashion and until Degas' own day was largely regarded as a medium suitable only for minor and ephemeral art. Degas owned several pastels by Maurice Quentin de La Tour which he was forced to sell at the time of his brother's bankruptcy in 1875, but his own involvement with the medium seems to have been triggered by the sale, also in 1875, of an important collection of pastels by Millet and by the advocacy of his friend, the Italian artist Giuseppe de Nittis. Degas claimed that pastel was easier on his fragile eyesight, but the medium also had several other advantages for him. Pastel is a far more rapid medium than oils and thus lent itself to Degas' restless and experimental working methods. He soon discovered that pastel could be combined with other media, such as monotype and the quick-drying gouache and tempera. As pastel is an opaque medium it allowed him to superimpose layers of colour and to indulge his passion for reworking his pictures. Alterations and additions were also more easily made to the size of works on paper than on canvas (a work like *Dancers in the Wings*, which looks at first glance like a fragment of a larger work, was actually built up from ten separate pieces of paper). By constant experiment, Degas enormously extended the range of the medium, using it in all sorts of original and unexpected ways. In addition to the traditional sticks of pastel, he would use pastel dust mixed with water as a paint to be applied with brushes. He would blur colours with the aid of steam, his fingers, rags or the traditional 'stump' (a finger of rolled paper). Despite the inherent opacity of pastels, Degas was able to obtain effects of shimmering iridescence. By laying striations of colour over contrasting underlayers, he produced pastels in later years which compare with the most dazzling oil paintings of the Impressionists for richness of colour. Degas' exploration of the medium of pastel seemed to liberate his sense of colour, rather as Turner's use of watercolour earlier in the century had led him to the luminous effects which we see in his late oil paintings.

Experimentation with unconventional techniques also characterized Degas' important and prolific activity as a graphic artist. In all, he made over sixty etchings and lithographs. He made his first etching as early as the mid-1850s under the tuition of a certain Prince Soutzo, an amateur artist and friend of his father. He took further instruction in print-making techniques from Félix Bracquemond, a print-maker who is chiefly remembered today for his pioneering enthusiasm for Japanese woodcut prints. In the late 1870s and 1880s, Degas collaborated with Pissarro and Mary Cassatt on experiments in graphic art. The following extract from a letter from Degas to Pissarro offers a fascinating insight into Degas' working methods and illustrates his passion for the technical aspects of print-making:

My dear Pissarro, I compliment you on your enthusiasm; I hurried to Mademoiselle Cassatt with your parcel. She congratulates you as I do in this matter.

Here are the proofs: The prevailing blackish or rather greyish shade comes from the zinc which is greasy in itself and retains the printer's black. The plate is not smooth enough. I feel sure that you have not the same facilities at Pontoise as at the rue de la Huchette. In spite of that you must have something a bit more polished . . .

This is the method. Take a very smooth plate (it is essential, you understand). Degrease it thoroughly with whitening. Previously you will have prepared a solution of resin in very concentrated alcohol. This liquid, poured after the manner of photographers when they pour collodion on to their glass plates (take care, as they do, to drain the plate well by inclining it) this liquid then evaporates and leaves the plate covered with a coating, more or less thick, of small particles of resin. In allowing it to bite you obtain a network of lines, deeper or less deep, according to whether you allowed it to bite more or less. To obtain equal hues this is necessary; to get less regular effects you can obtain them with a stump or with your finger or any other pressure on the paper which covers the soft ground.

Your soft ground seems to me to be a little too greasy. You have added a little too much grease or tallow.

What did you blacken your ground with to get that bistre tone behind the drawing? It is very pretty.

Try something a little larger with a better plate.

With regard to the colour I shall have your next lot printed with a coloured ink. I have also other ideas for coloured plates . . . .

Be of good cheer, DEGAS

Degas' notebooks too are full of similar recipes and instructions and addresses where he could find special materials or help with some aspect of print-making techniques. His friend, the artist and engraver Marcellin Desboutin, described how in the summer of 1876, when Degas was experimenting with the printing of monotypes on zinc and copper plates he was 'running all over Paris – in this heat – to search out the industrial enterprise relevant to this obsession.' Degas was like a medieval alchemist in his restless searching and unconventional improvisatory methods. One of his discoveries was the so-called 'electric crayon', in fact the filament from an electric light bulb, which he used to incise fine lines in his etchings. Just as many of his contemporaries believed that he ruined his pictures through his obsession with re-working, there were those who thought that his success as a print-maker was thwarted by his constant experimentation. Renoir's friend, the art critic Georges Rivière, said, 'If Degas had only been content to draw his plate quite straightforwardly, he would have left us the finest prints of the nineteenth century.' It could be said that Degas as print-maker remained an inspired amateur. Professional print-makers of his day disapproved of the way in which

Degas, *Woman Standing in a Bathtub*, c1879–85. Musée d'Orsay, Paris.

Degas seemed to break all the rules. Renoir told Vollard that he used to watch the printer Cadart pulling impressions from Degas' plates, 'I don't dare say etchings – people laugh when you call them that. The specialists are always ready to tell you that they're full of tricks . . . that the man didn't know the first principles of aqua-forte. But they're beautiful, just the same.' It was, in fact, in Degas' ignorance of the 'rules' and his determined improvisation that his strength and originality as a print-maker lay.

Degas, *After the Bath*, c1896. Philadelphia Museum of Art.
Purchased: Estate of the late George D. Widener.

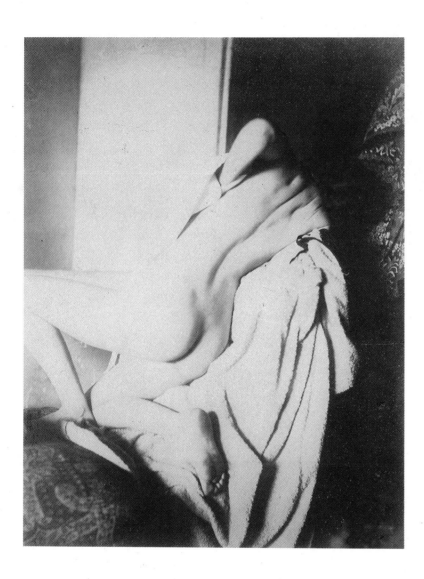

After the Bath, 1896, photograph by Degas. Collection of the J. Paul Getty Museum, Malibu, California.

Some of Degas' most personal works were made by the unusual technique of monotype. The monotype was invented in the seventeenth century, although its expressive potential was not developed until Degas took up the technique in the 1870s. Monotype is a method by which one impression can be printed from a drawing in greasy ink made on a metal or glass plate. Occasionally, a second or even a third weaker image can be taken from the image. One might ask why any artist should wish to use a graphic technique which cannot produce multiple images rather than drawing directly on paper. Degas no doubt enjoyed the fluency and freedom of drawing in brush on a non-absorbent surface. He was also able to create tones and textures of an extraordinary subtlety and suggestiveness, quite different from the effect he would have obtained by drawing in brush and ink on paper. He was probably also stimulated by the psychological 'distancing' involved in the reversal of the image in the process of printing. As an alternative to drawing with the brush on the plate or sometimes in combination with it, Degas could ink the plate and draw through the ink in negative. This method produced a sensuous, velvety effect, particularly lovely and mysterious in some of his depictions of the nude.

Another interesting technical aspect of Degas' art is his use of photography.

It has already been pointed out that many of Degas' pictures of the 1870s have the look of snapshots and that some of his more innovative compositional devices – high viewpoints, asymmetry and the cutting and overlapping of figures – have their origin in both photography and Japanese woodcut prints. As well as exploring the kind of effects found in photographs, Degas is believed to have based a number of his pictures directly on photographs, going back to *The Woman with the Chrysanthemums* of 1865 and *Sulking*. Like many nineteenth-century painters, Degas may have been keen to suppress the evidence of his use of photographs at least in the early years of his career. Definite proof exists in only a small number of cases, such as the small portrait of Princess Metternich based on a visiting card, and the drawings of cantering horses taken directly from photographs by Eadweard Muybridge. By the early 1890s, Degas owned a camera which clearly afforded him a great deal of pleasure. He took a number of photographs of friends, which are as carefully posed to look natural and casual as his earlier paintings. Some of these photographs are very beautiful and can be regarded as works of art in their own right. Around 1896, Degas made a series of pictures of an awkwardly positioned nude drying herself after a bath which are clearly based upon a still-existing photograph which was most probably taken by himself.

Amongst the many photographs taken of Degas by other people is a particularly poignant one dating from 1885, in which he and his friends recreate the composition of Ingres' *Apotheosis of Homer*, with Degas taking the position of the blind poet. Another, taken by Count Giuseppe Primoli in 1889, catches Degas in a pose as unconscious and intimate as those of the female nudes depicted in the 1880s. It shows Degas adjusting his trousers as he leaves a public urinal. His gesture is partly hidden by a top-hatted man passing him on the way into the urinal – a neat example of overlapping which looks like one of his own compositions. The irony was not lost on the artist, who wrote to the photographer to thank him, saying, 'Without the person arriving I would have been caught buttoning my trousers ridiculously, and everyone would have laughed.'

In the 1890s, Degas continued with his favourite themes of dancers, bathers and jockeys. In addition to these and the occasional portrait, he developed a belated and unexpected interest in landscape. His first one-man show, which took place at Durand-Ruel's gallery in 1892, consisted of an extraordinary series of mysterious, semi-abstract colour monotypes of landscapes made from memory or imagination.

Although many of Degas' themes and sometimes even the poses of the figures remained the same, his style changed radically after 1890. Pictures became larger and figures still larger within them. When he would once have

Apotheosis of Degas, parody of Ingres' *Apotheosis of Homer*, 1885, photograph. Bibliothèque Nationale, Paris.

shown a whole company of dancers on stage, he would now show part of the bodies of three or four seen from close-to. Throughout the 1890s his drawing and his colour became increasingly bold. These changes were to a certain extent forced upon Degas by his worsening eyesight. He had been haunted by the fear of blindness since he first had trouble with his eyes during the Franco-Prussian War in 1870–71. In later years he referred to these fears with obsessive frequency in his letters and conversations. Encroaching blindness did not seriously interrupt the flow of masterpieces until after 1900 and even in the final years of his career he was able to produce images of extraordinary power. In a curious way, Degas' poor sight helped to heighten his sensibilities as Beethoven's deafness had increased his muscial powers. Renoir maintained that 'Degas painted his best things when his sight was failing.' Degas himself explained the mystery of his late work in another way: 'It is very good to

Degas leaving a public lavatory, 1889, photograph by Count Giuseppe Primoli. Bibliothèque Nationale, Paris.

copy what one sees; it is much better to draw what one can no longer see except in one's memory. It is a transformation in which imagination and memory work together. You only reproduce what struck you, that is to say the essential. That way, your memories and your fantasy are freed from the tyranny of nature.'

Although the increasing subjectivity of Degas' art may have been forced upon him by blindness, it also brought him in line with many younger avant-garde artists, particularly those associated with the Symbolist movement who, in the last two decades of the nineteenth century, were also seeking to escape from 'the tyranny of nature.' The delicate poetry of Degas' monotype landscapes has

more in common with the fantastic dream world of Odilon Redon than with the stolid realism of Pissarro's late landscapes or with Monet's increasingly fanatical attempts to fix effects of light and colour at particular times of the day. The almost hallucinatory colours of Degas' ballet scenes in the 1890s remind one strongly of Redon, an artist whom Degas admired, although he claimed that he was unable to understand what Redon's art was about.

Degas frequently claimed in later years that he wished he had worked entirely in black and white. It was in these years, however, that his colour, freed from naturalistic considerations, achieved its greatest beauty and intensity. By hatching one brilliant colour into another in the backgrounds of his late *toilettes*, Degas often created an effect of almost oriental luxuriousness. It is perhaps no coincidence that in the 1890s he developed an enthusiasm for the *Arabian Nights* and for oriental carpets.

Deteriorating eyesight also drove Degas increasingly to sculpture. 'Now that my sight is leaving me,' he told Vollard, 'I must take up a blind man's craft.' Working in wax, Degas seemed to take a perverse delight in the impermanence of his sculptures. When Vollard was disappointed at the destruction of an exquisite statuette of a dancer, Degas told him triumphantly, 'All you think of, Vollard, is what it was worth, but I wouldn't take a bucket of gold for the pleasure I had in destroying it and beginning all over again.' To the critic Thiebault-Sisson he explained in more detail, 'The only reason that I made wax figures of animals and humans was for my own satisfaction, not to take time off from painting or drawing, but in order to give my paintings and drawings greater expression, greater ardour, more life. They are exercises to get me going; documentary, preparatory motions, nothing more. None of this is intended for sale.'

In sculpture, as well as in print-making, Degas re-

Degas, *Dancer Looking at the Sole of her Foot*, 1910–11. The Tate
Gallery, London.

mained an inspired amateur, ignoring the recipes of the 'professionals'. His bold improvisations and experiments sometimes led to disaster but sometimes also to solutions of extraordinary originality. Renoir believed Degas rather than Rodin to be the greatest sculptor of the day and on one occasion went so far as to declare, 'Since Chartres there has been only one sculptor, in my view, and that is Degas.'

Perhaps Degas' greatest solace in this time of encroaching blindness and isolation was his art collection. He was forced to sell his first collection at the time of his family's financial difficulties in 1875, but from about 1890, the high prices fetched by his own work enabled him to indulge his passion for collecting.

Like any true collector, Degas was compulsive and prepared to make any financial sacrifice for the sake of his collection. Daniel Halévy remembered him proudly showing off his new pictures and saying, 'Here is my new Van Gogh and my Cézanne. I go on buying and buying! I can't stop.' The arrival of a new work by Delacroix or Ingres was a cause for great celebration. Vollard describes Degas' pleasure in hunting out treasures and how on one occasion, when a painting by Delacroix was delivered during lunch, Degas' aged house-keeper announced, 'Monsieur, the Delacroix is coming up!' and Degas rushed out to meet it, 'without even taking time to remove the napkin from his collar.' Degas' collection was remarkable for its quality and for the catholic tastes which it displayed. Amongst the old masters represented were El Greco (a painter only just beginning to be appreciated in Degas' day), Tiepolo and Cuyp. He was particularly proud of the many works which he owned by Ingres and Delacroix. According to Lemoisne, he owned 33 drawings by Ingres and 20 paintings, including four of his finest portraits. Although Degas was not much attracted to the medium of watercolour, he owned around 60

watercolours and drawings by Delacroix and a number of oils, including the portrait of Baron Schwiter and Delacroix's copy of Rubens' *Henry IV Giving the Regency to Marie de Medici* and the sketch for *The Battle of Nancy*. There were numerous Japanese woodcut prints, thousands of lithographs by Daumier and Gavarni and virtually the complete graphic works of Manet. There were exquisite landscapes by Corot, and, amongst his contemporaries or near contemporaries, works by Manet, Puvis de Chavannes, Whistler, Millet, Pissarro, Renoir, Sisley, Morisot, Cassatt and Valadon. The most significant absentee was Monet, an artist for whom Degas had little sympathy, although he did admire the series of paintings of Rouen cathedral. Nevertheless, Degas had a remarkable ability to understand the work of younger or more 'advanced' artists such as Cézanne, Gauguin and Van Gogh. Amongst works painted by Cézanne, he owned a self-portrait, a portrait of the collector Victor Chocquet, some fine still-life paintings and a small picture of Venus and Cupid. Pissarro described how

Degas, *Seated Dancer, View of Profile From the Right*, 1873. Cabinet des Dessins, Musée d'Orsay, Paris.

Degas in Bartholomé's garden, c1908, photograph by Bartholomé.
Bibliothèque Nationale, Paris.

Degas was 'seduced by the charm of this refined savage' when Vollard showed Cézanne's paintings in 1895 and how Degas and Renoir had to draw straws for a still-life which they both wanted. Degas was the only member of the older circle of Impressionist artists who fully appreciated the talent of Gauguin, despite the fact that the two had clashed at the time of the seventh Impressionist exhibition, from which Gauguin had been partly re-

sponsible for Degas' exclusion. Unable to comprehend Degas' enthusiasm for Gauguin, Pissarro suspected that he merely wanted to help out financially when he bought several works, including *La Belle Angèle* and *Hina Tefatu (Moon and Earth)*. Touched by Degas' support, Gauguin wrote in 1898, 'In his talent and his behaviour, Degas offers a rare example of what the artist ought to be . . . one has never heard of or seen, on his part, any dirty trick, indelicacy, or unworthy action of any kind. Art and dignity!' Perhaps the greatest surprise was that Degas owned a *Sunflowers* and a still-life with fruit by Van Gogh, an artist whose emotionalism and handling of paint would seem to be thoroughly alien to Degas. Degas had planned to leave his collection as a museum, but seems to have changed his mind after a visit to the gloomy Musée Gustave Moreau, and his glorious collection was dispersed in a series of sales after his death.

Degas continued to battle against blindness and to work until about 1912, the year in which he was forced to move from the apartment in the rue Victor-Massé, where he had lived for a quarter of a century. This was a blow from which he never really recovered. His last years were sad; he was indifferent to his own increasing fame and to the events in the world around him. In the words of Vollard, 'Gradually he sunk into a dream, and would inquire, "Well, how is the war going?" in the same tone that he would ask Zoë, "Where is my tea?" ' Degas died on 27 September 1917. By this time, his work was universally acknowledged as one of the greatest glories of France, but in the midst of the First World War, at a moment when France seemed to be on the verge of collapse, Degas' death passed almost unnoticed. It was perhaps a fitting end for a men who had once said, 'I would like to be illustrious and unknown!'

THE PLATES

Portrait of the Artist, 1855

81 × 64cm. Musée d'Orsay, Paris

If youthful self-portraits by Degas, Fantin-Latour, Frith, Munch, Picasso and Max Ernst are compared, a curious family resemblance becomes apparent between these artists whose mature work has so little in common. The resemblance lies chiefly in a facial expression which is wary, searching and slightly tentative.

There are artists such as Rembrandt and Munch who made self-portraits throughout their careers as a kind of diary or autobiography, but the majority date from early on in artists' careers. Many artists abandon painting self-portraits after they have reached artistic maturity. It is as if the making of them were a necessary part of establishing an artistic identity.

Degas painted at least fifteen self-portraits, all in the early years of his career before he had developed into a painter of modern-life subjects. The present portrait was painted early in 1855, when Degas was about 20 years old. For the work of a young student newly enrolled at the École des Beaux-Arts, it is of impressive quality and compelling intensity. The only sign of youthful inexperience is in the clumsy drawing of the left hand. At the same time it is a conservative painting with no hint of future radical tendencies. Degas' debt to his hero Ingres in this picture has frequently been pointed out and the pose follows almost exactly that of Ingres in his own youthful self-portrait of 1804, which Degas would have seen at the Musée Condé at Chantilly. It was at just about this time that Degas was introduced to Ingres by his friends, the Valpinçons, and he would have been able to study a large part of Ingres' œuvre at the Paris Universal Exhibition of 1855. Unlike Ingres, who in general preferred light-toned background for his portraits, Degas has chosen to surround himself by old-masterish gloom. The picture also differs from Ingres' and his own mature portraits by concentrating almost entirely upon the face and omitting accessories.

The full lips and dark, heavy-lidded eyes betray Degas' Mediterranean ancestry and the sensuality which was an important part of his personality, although subjected to rigid control throughout his long career.

Roman Beggar Woman, 1857

100.3 × 75.2cm. City Museum and Art Gallery, Birmingham

This meticulously observed study of an old beggar woman was painted during Degas' first visit to Rome. He arrived there in October 1856 and remained for the best part of two years (with a three-month break in the middle spent with his family in Naples). Much of his time in Rome was spent studying and copying the old masters in churches and the Vatican Museums, something which was considered an essential part of any artist's education in the nineteenth century. He also filled numerous sketch books with his observations from Rome's busy and colourful street life.

There had been a tradition of picturesque genre painting in Rome which went back to the Bamboccianti, a group of Dutch and Flemish painters who lived in the city in the seventeenth century. The tradition was consciously revived in the 1850s with the encouragement of Victor Schnetz, the director of the French Academy in Rome. Many of Degas' friends and contemporaries painted pictures of Italian beggars and peasants. Degas himself soon tired of a subject which had become somewhat clichéd and already the following year wrote dismissively in a note book, 'I'm not mad about the famous picturesqueness of Italy.' What touched him, he said, was not trivial genre but the eternal element to be discovered in what he saw around him. This attitude had perhaps already influenced the way in which he treated the subject of the old woman. Degas' picture completely lacks both the sentimentality and picturesque setting of contemporary academic genre scenes and also any element of social comment or protest which might have been present in the depiction of such subjects by the older French Realists such as Daumier or Courbet or by English painters such as Henry Wallis and Ford Madox Brown.

The simple and severe composition is dominated by vertical and horizontal lines, with the old woman seen in strict profile, giving the painting a gravitas not often found in genre scenes.

Although more classically composed and more thinly painted, Degas' *Roman Beggar Woman* anticipates Manet's Velazquez-inspired treatment of similar subjects in the early 1860s. Degas himself never returned to this type of low-life subject, preferring instead to concentrate on the depiction of various kinds of young working women.

Portrait of Hilaire Degas, 1857

53 × 41cm. Musée d'Orsay, Paris

Degas painted this small and immaculate portrait of his grandfather in the summer of 1857 when he was staying with him in his villa at Capodimonte outside Naples. Degas held this grand old patriarch, who had founded the family fortunes, in the greatest respect and affection. At the age of 87, Hilaire was nearing the end of his long and eventful life. Born in Orléans in 1770, he began his career as a corn merchant. Narrowly escaping arrest and possible execution during the French Revolution, he fled to Naples, where by dint of hard work and good luck he was eventually able to found a bank and to marry into a wealthy Italian family. Degas' father was one of the ten children of this marriage.

This portrait, which Degas gave to his grandfather and which belonged to his Italian relatives until it was acquired by the Louvre in 1932, would probably have seemed quaintly old-fashioned to Degas' more adventurous contemporaries in Paris. The high degree of finish, crisp highlights, and its carefully calculated composition, in which the door and picture frames play an important part, are reminiscent of Ingres, who was and remained one of Degas' greatest heroes.

The Bellelli Family, 1858–67

200 × 250cm. Musée d'Orsay, Paris

The Bellelli Family is the most impressive and ambitious of the family portraits which preoccupied Degas during the first decade of his career. He made numerous and elaborate studies for this picture while staying in Florence in late 1858 and early 1859 with his aunt Laure de Gas and her husband Baron Bellelli, who had been exiled from Naples for his political activities. A particularly lovely and delicate oil study exists for Laure's hand resting upon the table. It seems likely that the painting was itself executed after Degas' return to Paris in 1859 and then extensively reworked at two later dates. Circumstantial evidence suggests that Degas exhibited the picture at the Salon of 1867, before which he made alterations and additions. After suffering damage (which can still be clearly seen above the Baron's head) the picture was repaired and re-worked again towards the end of Degas' career.

This complex portrait offers plentiful evidence of Degas' voracious and wide-ranging interest in the art of the past. Numerous old-master sources or influences have been suggested, including the grave and formal Genoese portraits of Van Dyck, which Degas greatly admired at the time, and portraits by Holbein and Pontormo, which he had copied, the elaborate group portrait drawings of Ingres and two great Spanish royal group portraits, Velazquez's *Las Meninas* and Goya's *Family of Charles IV* (neither of which he had seen in the original at this stage).

The modernity of this picture lies in the subtelty with which Degas expressed the tensions of a profoundly unhappy household. Several surviving letters from Laure to her nephew show the warmth of her affections for the painter, her hostility towards her husband and her feelings of melancholy and frustration. In one letter she wrote, 'You must be very happy to be with your family again, instead of being in the presence of a sad face like mine and a disagreeable one like my husband's', and in another, 'To live with Gennaro, whose detestable character you know, and with him having no serious occupation, is something which will soon drive me into my grave.' Degas shows the alienation of husband and wife through the posing and placing of the figures and the lack of physical or eye contact. Laure presents a particularly sombre figure in the black mourning which she was still wearing after the recent death of her father, Hilaire Degas, whose portrait in red chalk can be seen on the wall next to her head. The colour of the wallpaper, somewhere between blue, grey and green, contrasting with the warm, peachy flesh tones and the flat, unmodelled blacks, was a combination that particularly appealed to Degas at this period. The informal pose of the little girl in the centre, with a leg folded under her and the spaniel beheaded by the right edge of the picture, are characteristically unconventional touches.

Semiramis Building Babylon, c.1860–62

150 × 258cm. Musée d'Orsay, Paris

In 1860, the year in which Degas probably began work on this picture, the Paris opera put on several performances of Rossini's opera *Semiramis*. Degas, who was a great opera lover, may have been inspired by these performances to paint *Semiramis Building Babylon*. Unlike his later painting of Meyerbeer's *Robert the Devil*, this picture does not incorporate any elements of the actual opera production, nor does it have any theatrical ambiance.

During this period, Degas was attempting to revivify the genre of history painting which had become tired and clichéd in the hands of the artists most successful at the Salon, such as Bouguereau, Cabanel and Gérôme. This ambition set Degas apart from many of his more radical contemporaries and linked him instead to Puvis de Chavannes and Moreau, artists who were regarded as both eccentric and reactionary in the 1860s, but who became heroes to a later generation of artists in reaction to the materialism of the mid-nineteenth century and to the tenets of Realism and Impressionism. The serene mood of this picture and its frieze-like composition are reminiscent of the great murals that Puvis de Chavannes began to paint about this time, and the elaborate and fantastic city in the background would seem to show the influence of Gustave Moreau, with whom Degas was on terms of close friendship in the late 1850s.

Semiramis was a queen of ancient Assyria famous for her beauty and her cruelty. Moreau, who was fascinated by legendary 'femmes fatales', may well have encouraged Degas to choose the subject, although Degas did not sieze upon the darker aspects of the story.

Young Spartans, c.1860–62

109 × 155cm. National Gallery, London

The full title which Degas himself gave to this picture was *Young Spartan Girls Challenging Boys*. It is one of many pictures in the early years of his career which show tension between the sexes. The subject is taken from Plutarch's *Life of Lycurgus*, which describes how the young Spartan girls, according to Spartan law, were ordered to practise masculine sports and to engage in bouts of wrestling with boys. In the middle distance we can see Lycurgus and the Spartan mothers watching the contest.

The symmetrical composition and the arrangement of figures in groups parallel to the picture plane are relatively conventional. The subject, too, with its opportunities for the display of erudition and nudity, is, despite its obscurity, typical of the kind favoured by popular Salon artists. However, if one compared *Young Spartans* with Gérôme's *Young Greeks Cock Fighting*, exhibited at the Salon in 1847, it becomes evident just how personal and unconventional Degas' approach to history painting was. He leaves out all the archaeological and exotic accessories so dear to the Salon artists and public. His treatment of the nude is quite different too. His picture exhibits none of the slick eroticism of those of Gérôme, and whereas Gérôme followed Salon conventions by painting a smoothly curved, white-skinned female and a muscular, olive-skinned male, Degas does not differentiate so sharply between the sexes, painting both male and female as snub-nosed adolescents with skinny, angular bodies.

Degas retained a touching pride in this picture and continued to work on it. His reworkings are visible, especially in the heavy contours and numerous pentimenti in the left-hand group of girls. In later years, when most of the paintings in his studio were kept away from prying eyes, he would happily show this picture to visitors. As late as 1880, at the height of Degas' commitment to themes taken from modern life, he considered exhibiting *Young Spartans* publicly. It figures in the catalogue of the fifth Impressionist exhibition, although it seems that he did not actually show it in the end.

Portrait of the Artist, c.1863

92.5 × 66.5cm. Calouste Gulbenkian Foundation, Lisbon

The cubist painter, André Lhote, once described Degas as a 'disastrously incorruptible accountant'. It is an image of himself which Degas seems bent on promoting in several of his early self-portraits. With his top hat and frock coat, elegant chamois gloves, his polite gesture of greeting and his sober and humourless expression, this artist, who later delighted in shocking the bourgeoisie, seems himself to be the perfect bourgeois. Degas was, of course, from a thoroughly bourgeois background, but the same could be said of most nineteenth-century French painters. Amongst the great painters of that period, perhaps only Renoir and Daumier could really have claimed to have had working-class origins. Degas' bourgeois appearance in his self-portraits is not so much a matter of class as of generation. Degas and Manet (who cultivated a similarly bourgeois appearance) were reacting against the Romantic image of the artist as bohemian and rebel, which had been celebrated in Henri Murger's popular novel *Scènes de la Vie de Bohème*. It was an image which had been adopted not only by the overtly Romantic Delacroix (who painted himself as the doomed hero of Walter Scott's novel *The Bride of Lammermoor*) but by the ultra-conservative Ingres, who in his 1804 portrait showed himself with tousled hair, a coat thrown casually across his shoulders and the troubled expression of a poet, and by the realist Courbet, who depicted himself on various occasions as mad, wounded and as a kind of gypsy wanderer greeting his bourgeois patron as a man from another world. Degas' self-portrait may perhaps be making deliberate reference to Courbet's famous painting of his meeting with Alfred Bruyas, but the comparison only emphasizes how Degas eschews the confessional and self-dramatizing, and that he identifies with the bourgeois patron rather than with the bohemian artist. As in his self-portrait of 1855, Degas leaves out accessories and adds a background of a purely conventional kind.

Scene of Warfare in the Middle Ages (The Misfortunes of the Town of Orléans), 1865

81 × 147cm. Musée d'Orsay, Paris

The last of Degas' historical paintings was exhibited at the Salon in 1865 under the title *Scene of Warfare in the Middle Ages*, though it has become known as *The Misfortunes of the Town of Orléans*. No such massacre of women is recorded in the history of the French town of Orléans and it seems likely that the alternative title refers allegorically to New Orleans, where a branch of the Degas family lived and where the women folk had recently been mistreated by occupying Yankee troops in the American Civil War. It has been suggested that the traditional title resulted from a misreading of Degas' handwriting. 'Ville' (town) could easily be taken for 'Nlle.' ('nouvelle', or new, as Degas used to write it). *Scene of Warfare in the Middle Ages* is painted in Degas' favoured technique of *peinture à l'essence*, in which oil paints are diluted with spirits so as to remove their fatty and glutinous properties. The matt surface of the picture makes it hard to distinguish the medium and it has on occasion been mistakenly described as a pastel.

For its date, the composition is extraordinary bold and unconventional, anticipating many features of Degas' work of a decade later, such as the empty space in the centre, the figures pushed to the edges and in particular the horseman sliced in half by the right edge of the picture. The existence of a more centrally composed preliminary drawing and the fact that the right-hand piece of paper on which the picture is painted is reduced to a narrow strip might suggest that Degas cut the picture down at some later date.

Drawings also exist for the nude figures. They are amongst Degas' finest and are worthy of his hero Ingres in their sureness and economy of line.

Perhaps the most disturbing aspect of this picture is the voluptuousness of the female victims, whose poses are strangely similar to those of Degas' *toilettes* of the 1880s and 1890s. No wounds or blood are visible in this picture and it may be that the subject was largely an excuse for the depiction of female nudes in complicated and abandoned poses.

Jockeys in Front of the Grandstands, c.1866–68

46 × 61cm. Musée d'Orsay, Paris

Jockeys in Front of the Grandstands belongs to a group of early race-course pictures in which Degas shows the spectators as well as the jockeys and horses. The crowd here is smartly dressed and it has been suggested that the setting is Longchamp, the race-course in the Bois de Boulogne opened in 1857 as part of Baron Haussmann's scheme for urban renewal. Longchamp became a centre of fashion during the three short racing seasons there every year and had already inspired paintings by Manet. However, there are features which are inconsistent with Longchamp and as usual Degas is not overly concerned with topographical accuracy. As in the majority of his race-course scenes, *Jockeys in Front of the Grandstands* shows the moment before the race with just one recalcitrant horse in the distance disturbing the mood of calm. Flat, unmodulated areas of colour and tone, bounded by firm contours, suggest the influence of Japanese woodcut prints. Unlike contemporary works by Monet or Renoir, the picture was clearly painted in the studio and shows little interest in the accurate rendering of light and atmosphere, although the lengthening shadows indicate a time late in the day. The pronounced shadows, the carefully placed flag-pole, and the factory chimneys in the distance all play an important role in the design of the picture. Theodore Reff has shown that the central horse seen from behind was taken directly from Meissonier's painting *Napoleon III at the Battle of Solférino*. Degas has disguised his theft by reversing the image. There is a piquant irony in Degas making use of Meissonier, who was one of the artists most despised by Degas and his circle. Manet remarked maliciously of a Meissonier battle scene that everything looked as though it were made of steel, except the weapons. Degas himself dubbed Meissonier the 'king of the dwarves'. Meissonier painted tiny pictures whose minute detail made his bourgeois patrons feel that they were getting their money's worth. In real terms he probably earned more money per square inch of picture surface than any artist ever has. According to Zola, he could command 100,000 francs for each picture, at a time when Pissarro and Renoir were lucky to get a few hundred francs for some of their greatest masterpieces. Meissonier's fortune enabled him to construct a miniature railway in his garden so that he could chase and make accurate drawings of galloping horses. Degas never enjoyed or needed such an advantage. When he did not draw from memory or from small wax figures which he had modelled himself, he was quite happy to take his horses from photographs, English sporting prints or even despised academic painters.

James Tissot in an Artist's Studio, c.1867–68

151 × 112cm. Metropolitan Museum of Art, New York

Art historians have often puzzled over Degas' friendships with artists whose work seemed conventional and either in direct opposition to that of the Impressionists or else a bland dilution of it. Certainly Manet, Pissarro and Renoir were sometimes irritated by Degas' support of artists such as Raffaelli, de Nittis, Forain, Zandomeneghi and Tissot and his insistence on inviting them to exhibit with the Impressionists. In recent years changes in attitude have enabled us to develop a broader understanding of the extraordinary diversity of nineteenth-century French art and to judge these artists on their own merits, rather than rejecting them for not being fully Impressionist. In particular James Tissot, who was long dismissed as slick and trivial, has enjoyed a remarkable revival of interest.

Tissot had been a pupil of Degas' own teacher, Lamothe, in the mid-1850s, but the friendship dates from the early 1860s and lasted for the best part of fifteen years. At the time the portrait was painted Tissot was far more famous and successful than Degas. The sentimental and anecdotal aspect of his pictures and his minute attention to detail delighted the Parisian public and enabled him to build a magnificent house on a fashionable street. A few years later all this was lost when he was forced to flee to England after being compromised in the Paris Commune. The diarist Edmond de Goncourt remarked acidly upon the wealth of 'this ingenious exploiter of English idiocy', and recorded that he had a 'studio with a waiting room where, at all times, there is iced champagne at the disposal of visitors and, around the studio, a garden where all day long one can see a footman in silk stockings brushing and shining the shrubbery leaves.'

Tissot was known for his sartorial elegance. Degas shows him as a fashionable 'boulevardier' on a social visit. The top hat and overcoat beside him on the table, the walking stick clasped languidly between his fingers and his casual, somewhat unstable pose suggest that the visit is a brief one. Although Tissot would hardly be dropping in on his own studio in this way, Degas for the first time uses the sitter's surroundings to indicate his character and tastes. At the top of the portrait we see part of a large painting of a Japanese subject. The use of perspective in it shows that it is by a Western artist, perhaps by Tissot himself. Tissot was one of the first Parisian artists to be infected by the craze for Japanese art. Prominently placed in the centre of the picture is a copy of Cranach's portrait of Frederick the Wise, reflecting once again a common enthusiasm of Tissot and Degas for German Renaissance painting.

Tissot never owned this portrait, which remained in Degas' studio until his death. But its influence can clearly be seen in Tissot's brilliant portrait of Colonel Frederick Gustavus Burnaby, painted shortly afterwards.

Monsieur and Madame Edouard Manet, c.1868–69

65 × 71cm. Kitakyushu Municipal Museum of Art, Kitakyushu.

The mutilated state of this portrait bears eloquent witness to the turbulent relationship between Manet and Degas. In his short memoir of Degas, Ambroise Vollard recalled his explanation of how the picture came to be damaged:

Vollard: Who was responsible for cutting that picture?

Degas: It seems incredible, but Manet did it. He thought that the figure of Madame Manet detracted from the general effect, but I don't, and I'm going to try to paint her in again. I had a fearful shock when I saw it like that at his house. I picked it up and walked off without even saying good-bye. When I reached home I took down the little still-life he had given me, and sent it back to him with a note saying, 'Sir, I am sending back your plums.'

Vollard: But you made up with Manet afterwards, didn't you?

Degas: Oh, no one can remain at odds long with Manet. But the trouble is that he soon sold the plums. It was a beautiful little canvas . . . (*He paused*) Well, as I was saying, I wanted to restore Madame Manet to life and give the portrait back to him, but I have kept putting it off; and that is why you see it the way it is. I don't suppose I ever will get around to it now.

Interior, c.1868–69

81 × 116cm. Philadelphia Museum of Art, Philadelphia

Of the several pictures of the late 1860s which depict tension between the sexes, *Interior* is the most dramatic and mysterious. Degas creates a mood heavy with dark emotions and the threat of violence, without resorting to the exaggerated melodrama of Victorian pictures such as Egg's *Past and Present* or Luke Fildes' *The Doctor*. Unlike his Victorian contemporaries, Degas leaves his narrative ambiguous and relies upon subtle visual effects to build up the mood. The poses of the two protagonists, placed at either end of the composition, suggest frustration and despair (without recalling the gesticulations of bad actors as the figures in so many Victorian and Salon paintings do). The rushing perspective of the floor and the claustrophobic effect of the room, with its flowered wallpaper, help to build up the tension. Above all, the mood is created by Degas' marvellous rendering of light and shadow. The light from the table-lamp picks out the woman's bare shoulder, her work-box, the articles of clothing on the floor and the empty bed, with telling clarity. Shadow eats up the face of the woman and the looming shadow behind the man assumes a menacing presence (an effect which anticipates the psychologically fraught paintings of Munch in the 1890s).

It is not surprising that the painting came to be known as *The Rape* and art historians have inevitably looked for literary sources. The source which corresponds most closely with details in the picture is the scene in Emile Zola's novel, *Thérèse Raquin*, in which the lovers Thérèse and Laurent, having murdered her husband, are overcome by guilt and despair on their own wedding night.

Melancholy, c.1869

19 × 24.7cm. Phillips Collection, Washington

Melancholy is exceptional in Degas' œuvre for its mood of languid pathos. The mask of cool detachment which is usually worn by both Degas and his sitters has been dropped to show an expression of overt emotion – of intense yearning. The facial features, too, differ from those of either the stern-faced bourgois ladies of Degas' family portraits or the pert ballet dancers, laundresses and milliners who people his scenes of modern life. With her long nose, strong chin and sensuous lips, the model of *Melancholy* resembles the type of beauty made fashionable in England by Dante Gabriel Rossetti and his fellow Pre-Raphaelites.

Melancholy bears a striking similarity to certain drawings by Rossetti of his wife, Lizzie Siddall, slumped languidly in chairs and absorbed in her own profound melancholia and still more so to studies which Rossetti made around 1860 for the painting *Found* which show his model Fanny Cornforth in an almost identical pose. Degas would certainly have known of the work of Rossetti through his friends Tissot, Fantin-Latour and in particular Whistler, who was at this time a close friend and great admirer of Rossetti. Degas may even have met Rossetti, who in 1864 was taken to visit the studios of various Parisian artists, including those of Courbet and Manet. Rossetti's comments on modern French painting echoed in still more chauvinist form those of Degas on English painting, 'It is well worthwhile for English painters to try and do something now, as the new French School is simple putrescence and decomposition.'

It would be difficult to produce firm evidence of the direct influence of Rossetti's work, which had not been exhibited in France when *Melancholy* was painted. Most likely the Rossettian influence filtered indirectly through the work of other painters such as Millais and Whistler. Degas was familiar with Millais' painting *The Eve of St. Agnes* which had been exhibited in Paris in 1867 and whose heroine has a dreamy, Rossettian character. Degas repeatedly sent warm greetings to Millais in his letters to Tissot of the early 1870s. Above all, though, it was Whistler who was the most significant channel for Anglo-French influences. The brooding redheaded woman of Whistler's *Symphony in White No.1, The White Girl* and his *Symphony in White No.3* (of which Degas had made a rapid sketch) occupy a point midway between Rossetti's women and Degas' *Melancholy*.

Sulking, c.1869–71

32.4 × 46.4cm. Metropolitan Museum of Art, New York

This small and enigmatic canvas was painted at the height of Degas' interest in English painting, which he had discovered at the Paris Exhibition of 1867 and which continued to intrigue him into the early 1870s. Degas seems here to be attempting the kind of modern genre picture for which Victorian artists were known. A comparison of *Sulking* with Victorian paintings such as Augustus Egg's *Past and Present*, Holman Hunt's *The Awakening Conscience* or Orchardson's *The First Cloud* shows Degas' far more subtle and ambiguous treatment of the theme of tension between the sexes. The anecdotal element is played down and there is a complete absence of moralizing and sentimentality. He shows the mood of the man and woman through their 'body language' and their placing in the composition, instead of through exaggerated facial expression and theatrical gesticulation. The engraving by J.F. Herring of a steeplechase, which so ingeniously links the heads of the man and the woman, is an example of another kind of English art that interested Degas – the sporting print.

The English painter, Walter Sickert, who was a friend of Degas and one of the most important channels of Degas' influence in England, later painted a picture called *Ennui* which might be regarded as a variation on the theme of *Sulking*.

The Orchestra of the Opera, c.1870

56.5 × 46.2cm. Musée d'Orsay, Paris

The conventional dark palette of much of this picture and the relatively high degree of finish are contradicted by the unconventionality of the composition which at first glance seems to be quite arbitrarily cropped at the top and on the right-hand side. The bulky figure of the double-bass player on the extreme right would have fulfilled the traditional function of rounding off the composition and created a sense of stability had he been turned inwards towards the middle of the picture. By turning right and looking out of the picture he does exactly the opposite. Degas also takes perverse and witty delight in severing both the heads and feet of the dancers on stage. However casual and accidental the composition may seem, everything is calculated to the last degree. The diagonal lines of the various musical instruments echo and answer one another as inevitably as the melodic lines of a fugue.

Unusual viewpoints, asymmetry and the cropping of figures are all features that Degas could have learnt from Japanese woodcut prints or from photographs, but the direct inspiration for the composition seems to have come from the caricatures of Daumier. In particular, Daumier's lithograph of 1852, *The Orchestra During the Performance of a Tragedy*, shows a remarkably similar division of orchestra pit and brightly-lit stage, with only the lower halves of the actors' bodies visible. Degas' originality lay in borrowing all these features from popular or 'lesser' art forms and presenting them in the medium of oil paint as 'High Art'.

The Orchestra of the Opera is not so much a ballet picture as a group portrait. The principal figure in the centre foreground is Degas' friend, the bassoonist Désiré Dihau, for whom the picture was painted. Around Dihau are various members of the opera orchestra, all sharply characterized. In addition to the cellist Pilet, the flautist Altés and the double-bass player Gouffe, Degas included various other friends not connected with the orchestra, such as the singer Pagans (seen in the violin section immediately to the right of the harp) and the painter Piot-Normand (also playing a violin). Degas did not hesitate to rearrange the traditional positioning of the instruments for the sake of the composition.

In the box in the top left-hand corner, we are given a glimpse of the composer Emmanuel Chabrier (1841–94) who in his *Suite Pastorale* came close to creating a musical equivalent of Impressionism. Chabrier was also painted by Manet and Renoir and built up one of the most important early collections of Impressionist paintings.

The Orchestra of the Opera was inherited by Désiré Dihau's sister, Marie Dihau, of whom Degas also made a magnificent portrait, seated at her piano. In 1924, she ceded ownership of both pictures to the Musée du Luxembourg in return for a pension and the right to keep the pictures until her death.

Lorenzo Pagans and Auguste De Gas, c.1871–2

54 × 40cm. Musée d'Orsay, Paris

Although he showed it only to his innermost circle of friends, this small double portrait of the Spanish singer Lorenzo Pagans and Degas' father seems to have been highly valued by the artist, perhaps as much for sentimental reasons as for its aesthetic merits. Curiously, Degas seems never to have painted a portrait of his father alone, although he painted from memory several variations of the subject of Auguste De Gas listening to Pagans, long after the deaths of both his father and the singer.

Auguste De Gas' letters to Degas, when the artist was living in Italy in the late 1850s, show him to have been a man of warm affections and cultivated tastes, who encouraged his son's vocation with intelligent and well-informed advice on artistic matters. He was also apparently a great lover of music. Degas shows him as a frail and elderly man, haloed by the open music on the piano behind him and lost in rather melancholy reverie as he listens to the music.

Degas, who was himself passionately interested in music, painted several pictures of musicians in the years around 1870. As when he painted the bassoonist Désiré Dihau, Degas here pays particular attention to the correct rendering of the musician's fingers as he performs. The musical instrument too, with its mother-of-pearl inlay, is painted with minute care.

Dance Foyer at the Opera in the rue Le Peletier, 1872

32 × 46cm. Musée d'Orsay, Paris

Between the interruptions caused by the Franco-Prussian War and its aftermath in 1870–71 and his visit to New Orleans in 1872, Degas returned briefly to the theme of the ballet with this tiny and immaculate painting of a dance class. It sets the pattern for Degas' dance pictures over the first half of the 1870s, which are mostly of classes or rehearsals. These rehearsals took place in the old Opera House in the rue Le Peletier, which Degas continued to paint long after it was burnt down in 1873 and replaced by the splendid new Palais Garnier in 1875. Degas seems not to have liked the suffocatingly rich interiors of the new opera house and, indeed, the handsome but severe dance foyer, with its purple marble pilasters and gilded frieze, is the finest setting that he allowed in any of his dance pictures. As usual, none of his dancers are individualized, but the ballet master has been identified as Degas' friend, Louis Merante.

Dance Foyer was first exhibited in London in 1872 by the dealer Durand-Ruel. In the early 1870s, Durand-Ruel had opened a branch of his gallery in London in an attempt to establish a taste for modern French painting in England. No doubt Durand-Ruel calculated that *Dance Foyer* would be a relatively safe picture to put before the conservative English public. The picture was in fact warmly praised by the critic of the *Pall Mall Gazette* and found a buyer in the collector, Louis Huth. *Dance Foyer* has always been one of Degas' most popular pictures. The relatively high degree of finish would have satisfied early viewers and the picture lacks most of the more provocative features that characterize his later ballet scenes. The dancers do not have plebeian facial features, nor do they scratch, yawn or slouch in unladylike poses. If one excepts the piquant slice of leg and tutu glimpsed through an open door, none of the figures are cut by the edge of the picture or by architectural elements. The most radical features of the picture are the empty space in the centre and the placing of the empty chair in the foreground.

The pleasing harmony of this picture and the cool and sparkling rendering of light have frequently been compared with the work of the seventeenth-century Delft master, Vermeer. The dull ochres and delicate greys that dominate the picture are enlivened by the brilliant highlights of the dance-master's white suit, the edge of the music on the stand and by judiciously placed touches of black and brighter colours. The sharp yellow sash of the dancer at the bar relates to the dull yellows around her and the dull red of Degas' signature is picked up by the fan on the empty chair and the sash of the dancer to the right of the notice-board.

Woman with an Oriental Vase, 1872

65 × 34cm. Musée d'Orsay, Paris

In several letters, Degas complained that his time in New Orleans was largely taken up with making portraits of his family. On 27 November 1872, he wrote to a friend in Paris, 'The family portraits have to be done more or less to suit the family taste, by impossible lighting, much interrupted with models full of affection but a little lacking in respect and taking you far less seriously because you are their nephew or their cousin.' Apart from *Portraits in an Office, New Orleans*, which lies somewhere between a modern-life genre scene and an elaborate group portrait, the most impressive picture resulting from Degas' five months in New Orleans is the haunting and somewhat melancholic *Woman with an Oriental Vase*. There has been much discussion of the identity of the sitter for this portrait. We shall never know for certain, but it seems likely that she was Degas' cousin, Desirée Musson. The fact that Degas had seriously considered marrying her seven years earlier might account in part for the tense and rather sad mood of the portrait.

As a portrait, *Woman with an Oriental Vase* was highly unconventional in both composition and lighting. The sitter is displaced from her expected position in the centre foreground and our view of her is partly obscured by the looming shadowed forms of the chair and table and the vase of flowers whose silhouetted leaves cut dramatically across her pale bodice. Though our eye is drawn to the woman by the almost theatrically strong lighting of her figure, her facial features are partly eaten up by shadow. Typically for Degas, the sitter gazes not towards us nor towards the centre of the picture, but out beyond the nearby left edge of the picture, so emphasizing the asymmetrical and apparently casual character of the composition, and conveying a sense of alienation. The sumptuous vase, patterned table cloth, jewellery and cast-off glove are reminiscent of the accessories in the great bourgeois portraits of Ingres' later years. Like Ingres, Degas uses the accessories to produce a richly decorative effect, the mustard colour of the gloves creating a deliciously piquant contrast with the surrounding blues and greens of the vase and the table cloth. Degas' technique is considerably broader than that of Ingres. The jewellery on the table is rapidly sketched in black with blobs of gold and whitish colour to indicate the shimmering highlights.

Portraits in an Office, New Orleans, 1873

73 × 92cm. Musée des Beaux-Arts, Pau

In a letter of 1873 to the London-based artist, James Tissot, Degas wrote that this painting was intended for the London picture dealer, Agnew, and that he hoped that Agnew would 'place' the picture in Manchester, then the most important centre of the textile industry, adding, 'If a spinner ever wished to find his painter he really ought to hit on me.'

The Manchester plan came to nothing and instead the picture was first exhibited at the second Impressionist exhibition in 1876. The exceptional realism of the picture, with its marvellously precise rendition of the still-life elements, mollified many critics generally hostile to Degas' work and to that of the other Impressionists. Curiously, Émile Zola, whose novels seem to have so much in common with Degas' work at this time, took the opposite view of most contemporary critics and attacked the picture harshly. He wrote, 'The trouble with this artist is that he spoils everything when it comes to putting a finishing touch to a work. His best pictures are among his sketches. In the course of completing a work, his drawing becomes weak and woeful. He paints canvases like his *Portraits in an Office, New Orleans*, halfway between a seascape and a newspaper reproduction. His artistic perceptions are excellent, but I fear that his brushes will never become creative.' Several twentieth century critics have also disliked the picture, finding it dull and reactionary. It has acquired new interest in recent years as historians of Impressionism have turned away from a purely visual and formalistic approach to a more social historical one and have explored the way in which the Impressionists recorded and commented upon the changing urban environment. The picture has also fascinated young contemporary artists such as Stephen Conroy, several of whose recently exhibited works owe a profound debt to *Portraits in an Office, New Orleans*. What seems to have intrigued Conroy is the curious psychological dislocation of the picture. None of the respectably dressed bourgeois gentlemen seem to communicate with one another.

Portraits in an Office, New Orleans is exactly what the title says: it offers portraits of Degas' family and their business associates. It was the first of Degas' pictures to be acquired by a public collection when the Musée des Beaux-Arts in Pau bought it in 1878 for 2,000 francs. Although he had been forced to drop his asking price substantially, Degas showed an uncharacteristic delight in this first sign of official recognition. Writing to the man who had bought the picture for the museum, Degas said, 'I must thank you warmly for the honour which you have done me. I must also admit to you that this is the first time that a museum has honoured me, and this official recognition surprises and flatters me intensely.'

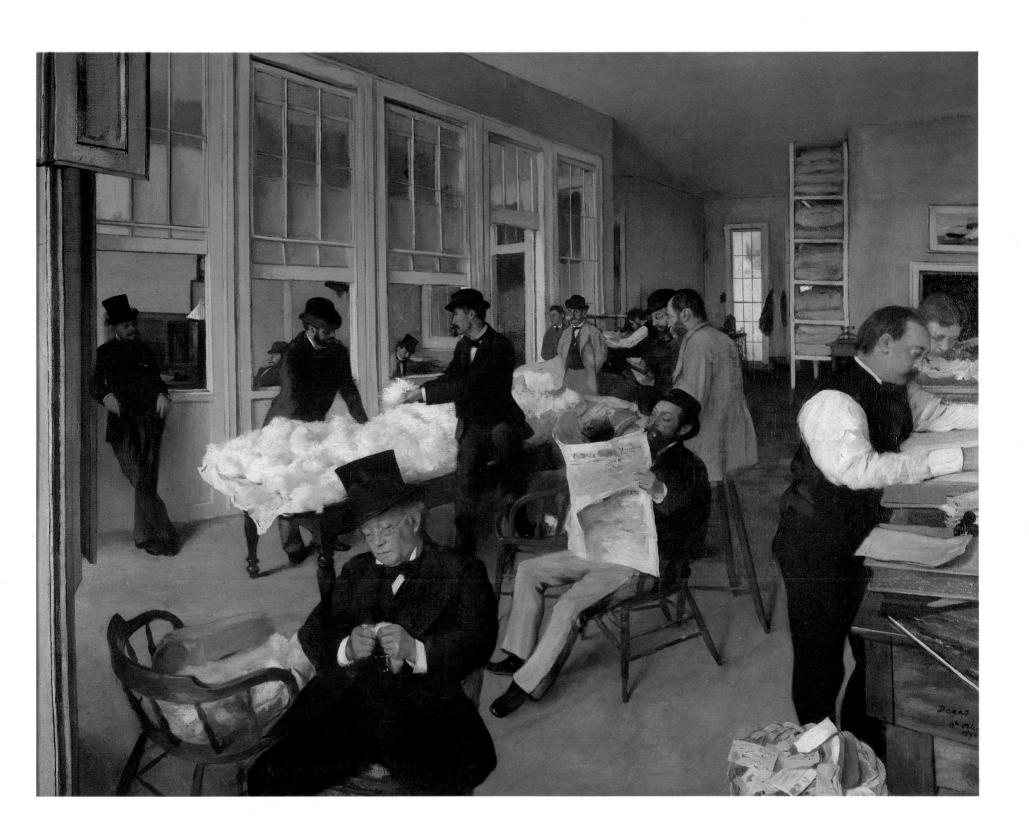

The Pedicure, 1873

61 × 46cm. Musée d'Orsay, Paris

The subject of this picture is unique in Degas' œuvre, and does not obviously belong in any of the groups of themes which preoccupied him during most of his career, although it might be described as a 'toilette without nudity'. There are a number of pictures by Degas in the 1870s in which he seems to have deliberately sought out the most unexpected, unpromising and – no doubt his more conventional contemporaries would have said – unpaintable subjects: a woman with a bandage around her head, a woman hanging from the roof by her teeth, or the Paris Stock Exchange. Although there would have been little precedent in Western art for this kind of subject unless treated in a humorous or anecdotal way, Degas may have turned once again to Japan for inspiration, and it has been suggested by Frank Whitford that this picture derives from a print by the Japanese artist Harunobu. Despite the banality of the subject, *The Pedicure* is a picture of great charm and delicacy and achieves a gravitas rare in such a tiny picture.

The Pedicure is painted on paper glued to canvas in the technique of *peinture à l'essence*. With this technique, which Degas used frequently, he was able to obtain effects of great delicacy and transparency.

The Pedicure, which is dated 1873, was probably painted early in the year, during the final month of Degas' long stay in New Orleans. As with his other pictures executed in New Orleans, there is no hint of his exotic surroundings and the picture might just as well have been painted in Paris.

Rehearsal of a Ballet on Stage, c.1874

54.3 × 73cm. Metropolitan Museum of Art, New York

Degas' ballet scenes convey a powerful sense of a reality observed and experienced, yet he never painted his pictures on the spot, from life, and frequently expressed his contempt for artists who were slaves to what they saw in front of them. Degas haunted the backstage areas of the Opera, made sketches from life and sometimes took photographs to aid his retentive memory. Like Watteau 150 years earlier, he built up a repertoire of poses, gestures and settings from which he constructed his compositions in his studio. He made frequent use of tracing paper to repeat, reverse, enlarge or recombine his figures in different compositions, producing countless variants. It was exceptional, however, for Degas to produce three almost identical pictures as he did with *Rehearsal of a Ballet on Stage*.

In each of the versions, the composition is basically the same, with intriguing minor variations. The monochrome version in oils belonging to the Musée d'Orsay lacks the tops of the musical instruments, dramatically silhouetted in the foreground of the other two versions. The dancing master and one of the two seated gentlemen on the right have been suppressed, although the ghostly presence of the latter is still visible beneath a transparent layer of paint. In the version illustrated here the dancer, bisected by the right edge of the picture, has been reversed so that she faces towards, rather than away, from us. Degas once again contrasts the grace of the dancers performing with the bored and inelegant poses of the others.

This particular version of *Rehearsal* has a strange and intriguing history which helps to explain both why he made three versions and why he used such an extraordinary mixture of media. It seems that the picture started as a pen and ink drawing which Degas submitted to the *Illustrated London News* for publication. The idea was not so outlandish when one remembers that Constantin Guys, the artist who had inspired Baudelaire's essay *The Painter of Modern Life*, had worked regularly for the *Illustrated London News*, and also that Degas at this period had hopes of achieving a substantial success in England, aided by Durand-Ruel, Tissot and Whistler. Degas' drawing was turned down, whereupon he worked over the original pen and ink drawing in his characteristic technique of *peinture à l'essence*, combined with some traces of watercolour, pastel and thicker oil paint. The other New York version also seems to have started as a pen and ink drawing and was perhaps made as a replica of this version when it was sent to London, before being reworked in pastel. The Musée d'Orsay version in oil on canvas seems to have been painted especially for exhibition and was shown in the first Impressionist exhibition in 1874.

The Dance Class, 1873–75

85 × 75cm. Musée d'Orsay, Paris

The Dance Class shows the rapid development of Degas' art since the relatively timid version of the same subject painted in 1870. Contact with the younger Impressionists had encouraged Degas to use a brighter palette. As usual, the dancers' sashes are used as an excuse to introduce bright spots of colour. The influence of Japanese woodcut prints may be seen in the sharply rising perspective of the floor as well as in the asymmetry of the composition. The greatest change, however, is in the sharper and more unflattering characterization of the dancers. Few of them seem to be taking much notice of the elderly ballet master. At the back of the room the seated dancers gossip with one another. A little nearer to us a dancer in a blue sash ostentatiously adjusts the arm of her dress. On the left we glimpse, between the two largest figures, another dancer reading a letter, the corner of which provides the lightest patch of tone in the picture. The depiction in an oil painting of the inelegant postures of the dancer seated with her legs apart and the dancer on top of the piano scratching her back would have been deeply offensive to a bourgeoisie obsessed with propriety. At the back of the room we see several mothers or chaperones, one of whom embraces a dancer in an unexplained emotional gesture.

The placing of the green watering can (upon which Degas signed his name) under the piano and the little dog sniffing the dancer's legs add further witty and iconoclastic touches to the picture.

The old man is Jules Perrot, a famous ballet dancer of an earlier generation, but by the mid-1870s long retired even as a choreographer and teacher. Degas painted Perrot several times. In the Burrell Collection's version of *Rehearsal for a Ballet on Stage* Perrot's figure is based upon a drawing from life which still exists. The appearance of Perrot in Degas' pictures is a reminder that male ballet dancers did exist in the nineteenth century, but Degas chose not to paint them, at least not while they were still young and active.

The composition of this picture evidently gave Degas problems. X-ray photographs reveal extensive alterations. The dancer in the foreground holding the fan has been superimposed on two earlier dancers in different poses, causing the paint on the fan to build up to an uncharacteristically thick and glutinous texture.

Absinthe, 1875–76

92 × 68cm. Musée d'Orsay, Paris

Absinthe is perhaps the harshest and most uncompromising of all Degas' depictions of Parisian low-life. It seems more than coincidence that its execution was exactly contemporary with the publication of Zola's novel, *L'Assommoir*, which dealt with alcoholism and prostitution with similarly harsh objectivity.

The two figures are known to have been posed for by Marcellin Desboutin and Ellen Andrée. Marcellin Desboutin was an etcher who occasionally exhibited paintings both at the Salon and with the Impressionists. He was a prominent member of the group of artists who met at the Café de la Nouvelle Athènes in the 1870s and at the time was one of Degas' closest friends. Ellen Andrée was an artist's model and actress who also appeared frequently at the Nouvelle Athènes. Degas seems to have taken a perverse delight in the uglification of this intelligent and pretty young actress, whose talent he admired and whose company he enjoyed over a period of many years. She appeared to better advantage in paintings by Manet and Renoir.

Ellen Andrée also posed for the more conservative artists who exhibited at the Salon, and most notoriously for the painting *Rolla* by Gervex, in which she once again appears as a courtesan. In Gervex's quasi-pornographic painting, which was rejected amidst great scandal by the Salon of 1878, she is presented as an extremely provocative nude. Not surprisingly, Ellen Andrée was not entirely happy about being immortalized by Degas as such a drab figure and later in life was given to making disparaging remarks about *Absinthe* and other Impressionist masterpieces for which she had posed.

The pale green liquid in the woman's glass and the nearby carafe of water identify her drink as absinthe, a drink as notorious in Degas' Paris as gin had been in Hogarth's London as a cause of working-class drunkenness and crime.

Aux Ambassadeurs, c.1876

37 × 27cm. Musée des Beaux-Arts, Lyon

Degas depicted the café-concerts of Paris over a short period in the late 1870s and early 1880s but they inspired some of his most memorable images. Amongst the enormous number of café-concerts, Degas favoured the relatively smart and expensive Café aux Ambassadeurs on the Champs-Elysées, where on warm summer evenings up to 1,200 people attended performances held in the open air, lit by globular gas lamps suspended from trees. *Aux Ambassadeurs* is once again drawn in pastel over monotype. The scratchy greys of the monotype are allowed to show through in many places, notably under the outstretched arm of the singer in red, adding to the density of the picture's texture and contrasting with the brilliant hues of the gas-lit dresses of the performers. *Aux Ambassadeurs* shares many visual devices with Degas' ballet scenes of the same period: the low viewpoint up to the stage, and the somewhat confusing depiction of space, the startlingly sharp transition between the dimly-lit audience in the foreground and the stage where forms are eaten up by shimmering light. The use of the dark silhouette of the double-bass, which Robert L. Herbert interprets as a 'symbol of manhood rising upward from the male orchestra' is so common in Degas' work of this period that it almost becomes a second signature. Naturally, the social milieu which Degas observes with great exactitude is very different from that of the opera house. The gaudy clothes of the three women in the foreground indicate that they are women of easy virtue, as are the women on stage behind the singer, who might use their bouquets and fans in a secret language of dalliance with male members of the audience.

At the Races, Gentlemen Jockeys, 1876–1887

66 × 81cm. Musée d'Orsay, Paris

At the Races, Gentlemen Jockeys was one of five pictures which Degas was commissioned to paint in 1874 by the baritone Jean-Baptiste Faure. Faure was one of the most important French opera singers of the nineteenth century, taking part in several notable premières, including those of Verdi's *Don Carlos*, Meyerbeer's *L'Africaine* and Ambroise Thomas's *Hamlet*. He also built up one of the most important early collections of Impressionist pictures, including several works by Manet, Monet and Sisley. It must have taken considerable courage and foresight to buy these artists' works when they were at their most notorious, though there were those who accused Faure of actually seeking notoriety by means of his collection. Faure's relations with Degas did not prove to be happy. Degas retrieved *At the Races, Gentlemen Jockeys* several times for major alterations and only completed it under threat of litigation in 1887, thirteen years after it was first commissioned. Despite the frustration of dealing with an artist as irritable and dilatory as Degas, Faure may have congratulated himself on having acquired one of Degas' finest and most characteristic paintings.

As in most of his race-course scenes, Degas presents us with the moment before the race and with what seems like a small fragment of reality, perceived in a fleeting moment. The momentary quality of the picture is accentuated by the train hurtling through the background, trailing clouds of smoke, and by the fact that none of the horses or figures are shown in their entirety. Despite its extreme asymmetry, the composition is splendidly harmonious and satisfying. X-rays have shown that what seems so casual and natural was only achieved after a painful process of alteration.

The jockey in the pink vest turning to the left is based on a drawing made in the late 1860s and of which Degas made use in several pictures. In this case, he has given him a rather portly torso to indicate that he is not a professional, but one of the gentlemen jockeys of the title.

Ballet Scene from 'Robert the Devil', 1876

76.6 × 81.3cm. Victoria and Albert Museum, London

The first version of *Ballet Scene from 'Robert the Devil'* originated, as did the earlier *Orchestra of the Opera*, to which it is closely related in composition, as an unconventional group portrait. Perhaps one should rather describe the picture as a portrait of a man surrounded by friends in a characteristic modern-life setting. The central figure of the first version, seen as though looking through a pair of opera glasses, is Degas' friend, the Parisian banker and collector Albert Hecht, who was also the first owner of the picture. In this version, Hecht has been moved to the extreme left of the composition and looks outwards to the left, reminding us that the picture is a small slice of life, and that life continues beyond the picture frame. Although the heads are not as strongly individualized as those of *Orchestra of the Opera*, it is possible to recognize the bassoonist Dihau once again in the orchestra pit and Count Ludovic Lepic, the friend who introduced Degas to the technique of monotype.

Degas gives the viewer a powerful illusion of sitting in the audience and looking across the orchestra pit and the silhouetted woodwind instruments up onto the gas-lit stage, which takes up a considerably larger portion of the picture surface than in *Orchestra of the Opera*. The picture shows Degas' fascination with the artificial lighting of the theatre. He faithfully renders artificial light from three separate sources: the desk lamps in the orchestra, which brightly illuminate the oddly shaped fragments of sheet music that we see through the tangle of heads in the foreground, the footlights, which eerily light the dancing figures from below, and gas lamps above the stage, intended to create an effect of moonlight.

The scene depicted on stage is from Meyerbeer's opera *Robert the Devil*, which had its première at the Paris Opera in 1831. In it the ghosts of nuns who have broken their vows of chastity rise from their tombs in a cloister and perform an orgiastic dance in order to corrupt the hero of the opera. Contemporary prints show that Degas has faithfully depicted the original sets for the scene, which became famous for its sensational visual effects.

The morbid and sensational aspects of Meyerbeer's opera were products of the Romanticism against which Degas, Monet and the Impressionists were consciously reacting. As opposed to the subjective emotionalism of the Romantics, Degas and his friends adopted a pose of cool and cynical objectivity. He distances us from the melodramatic goings-on on stage by the intrusion of banal reality in the foreground.

This version of the subject was commissioned by the famous baritone, Jean-Baptiste Faure. Although Faure never sang in this particular opera, he was closely associated with the composer, Meyerbeer. He frequently sang in Meyerbeer's operas *L'Etoile du Nord* and *Les Huguenots* and created the role of Nelusco in the première of *L'Africaine*.

The Star, 1876–77

58 × 42cm. Musée d'Orsay, Paris

The Star is executed in pastel over monotype. The scratchy monotype can be seen between the strokes of the pastel in the upper part of the picture. It was exhibited along with several other ballet pictures in the third Impressionist exhibition of 1877. It was in the mid-1870s that Degas became fascinated with the demanding graphic medium of monotype, by which a single print can be taken from an ink drawing made upon a blank metal plate. He seems to have been intrigued by the technical problems involved in the reversal in printing of the original image and also by the subtle and suggestive textures obtainable. Although the process of monotype allows only one strong clear impression, a second, weaker impression could be re-worked – something which Degas seems to have found extremely stimulating. As many as a quarter of Degas' pastels were made over a base of monotype.

The Star is one of the relatively rare ballet pictures by Degas which show an actual performance rather than a rehearsal. As in all his depictions of performances, elements of banal reality intrude upon the illusion created by the dancer. Her gracefulness is contrasted with the ungainly posture of the dancers standing in the wings and with the slightly sinister dark-suited gentleman (most probably her 'protector') glimpsed, minus his head, to the left of the picture. As in several depictions of performances we see the stage at an angle from a high viewpoint as though from a box and through opera glasses. The empty space in the lower part of the picture and the glow of light in the bottom-left corner help create a powerful impression of the dancer rushing towards the footlights to acknowledge the applause. It was a novel effect commented upon by the critics at the time.

The Star was acquired from Degas by the wealthy collector and talented amateur artist, Gustave Caillebotte. Although Caillebotte was one of those who opposed Degas' attempts to swamp the Impressionist exhibitions with his friends and followers, his collection contained seven pictures by Degas, which were amongst the first to enter a public collection when Caillebotte died in 1894, leaving his collection to the French nation.

The Madame's Birthday, 1876–77

26.6 × 29.6cm. Musée Picasso, Paris

The Madame's Birthday is drawn in pastel over one of the fifty or so monotypes which Degas devoted to the theme of the brothel in the late 1870s, and is the largest and most elaborated of three versions of the same composition. The delightful humour of this work lies in the contrast between the prostitutes, wearing only their stockings and shoes, and the matronly Madame, respectably dressed in widow's weeds and not entirely unlike Queen Victoria in appearance.

The subject of the brothel was popular with novelists of the 'Naturalist' school, such as Edmond de Goncourt, Zola, Huysmans and Maupassant, the style of whose writings Degas frequently seems to approach in his work during the 1870s.

These monotypes of brothels have been particularly admired by other artists for their honesty and marvellous economy of drawing. Renoir remarked to the dealer Vollard that 'when one approaches such subjects, it is often pornographic. One has to be Degas to give *The Madame's Birthday* an air of joyousness combined with the grandeur of an Egyptian bas-relief.' Picasso, who owned eleven of Degas' monotypes of brothels, was equally warm in his praise and towards the end of his life made a series of etchings inspired by them.

On the Beach, 1876

47 × 82.6cm. National Gallery, London

The subject of people enjoying themselves beside, on or in water was central to Impressionism. The movement was born beside the river Seine at the bathing resort of La Grenouillère in the summer of 1869: intrigued by the relaxed ambiance and by the play of light on water, Monet and Renoir both conceived the ambition to paint large-scale treatments of what seemed a fresh and typically modern subject. What came out of that summer was a series of small, loosely-brushed sketches made on the spot, which for the first time demonstrate all the main preoccupations and stylistic features of Impressionism. The artists tried to capture specific light and weather conditions in a specific moment at a specific place. Solid form and bounding contours are dissolved by light and atmosphere, which are rendered by means of small, broken touches of colour. Throughout the 1870s, Monet, Renoir and Sisley continued to paint boating and bathing scenes, which are amongst the most characteristic examples of Impressionism.

Degas' rare incursion into this kind of subject matter can only have served to underline the gulf between him and the other Impressionists when it was exhibited at the third Impressionist exhibition in 1877. Instead of the Impressionist weave of scintillating touches of colour, Degas paints with large flat areas of dull colour. Forms are heavily and clearly contoured. The figures, which cast no shadows, almost look like cut-outs. The woman in the foreground tenderly combing the young girl's hair, the shivering figures to the left, wrapped in towels, and the figures in the background gingerly stepping into the water, show Degas' remarkable powers of observation. He is, however, so indifferent to the Impressionist preoccupation with light, atmosphere and weather, that he allows the smoke from the two steamers in the distance to trail off in opposite directions. When someone asked Degas how he painted this picture, he answered, 'I spread my flannel vest on the floor of the studio, and had the model sit on it. You see, the air you breathe in a picture is not necessarily the same as the air out of doors.'

Dancer with a Bouquet, c.1877

40.3 × 50.4cm. Rhode Island School of Design, Providence

In the late 1870s, Degas frequently used the technique of pastel over monotype to rich and magical effect. The technique also facilitated Degas' penchant for making several variations on the same composition. This dancer, taking her applause at the front of the stage with her exultant face weirdly transformed by the fierce theatrical lighting from below, appears in at least four pastels. Three of them, including this one, are drawn over monotypes. In this version, which is the most complex and impressive, Degas has strikingly changed the original composition, which showed only the central dancer, by adding strips of paper to enlarge it and by introducing important new elements both behind and in front of her. We now seem to be standing in an opera box behind the woman in the foreground, whose wealth and elegance are indicated by her earring. We look down on to the stage over the top of her starkly silhouetted fan which cuts off the legs of the dancer. The introduction of the fan, as well as providing a startling visual effect, sets up a piquant tension between reality and the illusory world of the stage. The sudden jump between near and middle distance, creating a quasi-photographic effect like a snapshot, was probably inspired by Japanese woodcut prints such as Hiroshige's *Ferry at Haneda*, in which the Japanese artist has wittily framed an idyllic coastal landscape with a slice of hairy leg.

Women on a Café Terrace, Evening, 1877

41 × 60cm. Musée d'Orsay, Paris

Women on a Café Terrace, Evening, which is executed in pastel over monotype, shows prostitutes about their business of attracting passers-by on a busy, gas-lit boulevard. It could be a scene from a novel by Zola or the Goncourt brothers. Like Zola and the Goncourts, Degas has gone to great trouble to give a powerful and accurate impression of reality and has studied the costume, behaviour and gestures of his subjects as though he were a naturalist observing the mating rituals of gaudily plumed animals. In particular, the curious gesture of the woman putting her thumb to her teeth has the look of something observed from life. Robert L. Herbert, in his brilliant social history of Impressionism (*Impressionism Art, Leisure and Parisian Society,* Yale University Press, 1988) suggests that the woman bisected by a column, who seems to be getting out of her chair, may be answering a furtive invitation from the dark-suited bourgeois gentleman seen hurrying past on the right.

Once again, Degas makes brilliant use of the devices of cutting and overlapping of forms to create an illusion of actuality and instantaneity. The fact that the columns are cut off at top and bottom, and that we are unable to see how anybody or anything rests on the ground, helps to create a carefully calculated impression of confusion and spatial ambiguity.

Women on a Café Terrace, Evening was shown at the third Impressionist exhibition in 1877, where it attracted considerable attention because of its provocative subject matter. More than one critic saw the picture as a deliberate attempt to shock the bourgeoisie.

The Glove, c.1878

52.8 × 41.1cm. Fogg Art Museum, Cambridge, Massachussets

Degas presents us here with a close-up view of a café-concert performer as though seen through one of those opera glasses which artists of the Impressionist circles so often showed theatre-goers using.

Throughout his career Degas made careful study of the characteristic movements and gestures of the people he depicted. Here he has caught the way in which the singer raises her arm to emphasize the climactic note of her song. The great stars of the café-concert, such as Émilie Bécat and Thérésa, developed a special language of gesture. Gestures and inflections enabled them to put across sexual and political meanings which had escaped the censors, to whom all songs performed at the café-concerts had to be submitted. Degas was a great admirer of both Émilie Bécat and Thérésa, depicting Bécat several times and saying of Thérésa 'she opens her huge mouth and out comes the grossest, the most delicate, the most wittily tender voice there is.' We can well imagine that *The Glove* was inspired by one of these great café-concert artsts.

The striking combination of black and dull pink brings to mind the work of Degas' old friend, Edouard Manet. Their love of and effective use of black was one of several things which separated Degas and Manet from the younger Impressionists. Degas' superbly economical drawing of the black glove is an example of a love of eloquent silhouette which we also find in Manet's drawing of the barmaid's corseted torso in the *Bar at the Folies-Bergères* or the cat in *Olympia*.

Jockeys Before the Start, c.1878–80

107.3 × 73.7cm. Barber Institute, Birmingham

This startlingly asymmetrical composition seems to break with every traditional rule of Western art. So 'wrong' does the composition look to Western eyes that the viewer might believe that it had been composed arbitrarily or was a kind of snapshot carelessly taken with a Kodak camera. Far from being a casually observed slice of life painted on the spot, the picture was carefully composed in Degas' studio. Perhaps it would be more accurate to say that it was 're-composed', as most of the elements in it were taken from a picture painted about ten years earlier, with which Degas was evidently dissatisfied as it was found in a heavily repainted state in his studio at the time of his death. The seemingly accidental features of the first version are seized upon and emphasized in the second. In both versions Degas uses his characteristic devices of cropping and overlapping so that no horse is completely visible. In the second version Degas opens up a disturbingly large empty space on the left of the picture. The most disconcerting feature of this version is Degas' use of the vertical of the starting pole, placed to the right of centre and cropped at top and bottom, so that the viewer has difficulty locating it in the space of the picture. This, together with the minimal use of tonal gradation in the grass and the lack of any line or features to lead the eye into the distance, creates a powerful tension between flatness and three dimensionality.

If one compares *Jockeys Before the Start* with the Japanese artist Yoshitoshi's woodcut *A Poem by Abe No Nakamaro* one finds many of the same features – the use of the empty space, the asymmetrically placed vertical, the tension between flatness and three-dimensionality and even the curious celestial disc in the top-hand corner. There is no question of direct influence. Yoshitoshi's print actually dates from a few years after Degas' picture. By this time, however, Degas had so thoroughly absorbed the principles of Japanese composition that it is not necessary to look for specific borrowings.

Although Degas was as a rule far less interested than the Impressionists in painting effects of outdoor light and atmosphere, his rendering of the pale sunlight dimly penetrating wintry mists in this picture is particularly magical. It was an effect which fascinated the critic Armand Silvestre, who wrote of the picture's 'semi-lunar radiance' when reviewing the fourth Impressionist exhibition in which it was first shown.

Jockeys Before the Start is almost as original and surprising in its technique as in its composition. For what was the second largest race-course scene he ever made, Degas chose to paint not on canvas but on paper in a mixture of oil and 'essence' with touches of pastel.

Miss La La at the Cirque Fernando, 1879

117 × 77.5cm. National Gallery, London

In a period when women were supposed to be the 'weaker sex' – frail creatures imprisoned in whalebone corsets, whose legs were permanently hidden under enormous quantities of heavy petticoats and skirts which made physical exertion almost impossible, the sight of a woman swinging by her teeth from the roof of a circus must have seemed even more extraordinary than it would today. Miss La La, the subject of the picture, was a Mulatto trapeze artist who caused a sensation when she appeared at the Cirque Fernando in Paris in 1879. She gained the name of 'La Femme Canon' from her ability to hang upside down from the trapeze holding a chain between her teeth from which a canon was suspended, and which was then fired. Another part of her act consisted of being pulled up to the ceiling by means of a rope which she hung onto by her teeth.

It was around this time that Degas was most interested in unusual viewpoints. Having experimented extensively with high viewpoints, he wrote in one of his notebooks that he would like to tackle figures seen from below. Miss La La hanging from her rope provided the perfect opportunity. Degas watched her performance on at least four evenings, making careful drawings of both performer and architectural details of the setting. His several drawings show how careful he was to capture the right pose to convey a sense of precarious balance and vertiginous ascent. The placing of the figure in the top left-hand corner also helps to convey the feeling of dizzy heights. Unless the viewer is also hanging from a rope the viewpoint is presumably possible only through a pair of opera glasses.

Though painted in oils, the picture seems like a drawing. The brush is used to delineate contours almost as if it were a stick of charcoal. The paint surface is thin and matt with a slightly thicker and more sensuous application allowed only for the shimmering highlights of Miss La La's costume.

Miss La La at the Cirque Fernando was shown at the fourth Impressionist exhibition of 1879, along with several others of Degas' greatest masterpieces, such as the portraits of Duranty, Martelli and Michel-Lévy. Degas' magnificent contribution to the show, which marked a high point in his career, was sourly reviewed by Albert Wolff, the influential critic of *Le Figaro*, who wrote, 'M. Degas too used to have some talent, and his sketches are not just anybody's work, no doubt of that. If they were signed by a young man of twenty, one could confidently predict a future for him. But now he is past the apex of his career, without having taken a step forward . . . The misfortune of this school is that it refuses to learn, that it makes a principle out of ignorance and a theory of art out of its studio daubings . . .'

Portrait of Henri Michel-Lévy, 1879

41.5 × 27.3cm. Calouste Gulbenkian Foundation, Lisbon

This enigmatic and slightly sinister portrait is one of several that Degas made of fellow artists (Manet, Cassatt, Tissot, Bonnat and Moreau amongst them) and one of eight remarkable portraits that he showed at the fourth Impressionist exhibition in 1879. He has adopted his favourite devices of a high viewpoint and a looming object in the foreground (in this case the artist's paint box), which masks the subject's feet and obscures our perception of his precise position in space.

Henri Michel-Lévy had been painted by Degas eleven years earlier in an almost identical pose in the *Interior* of 1868. That picture (also known as *The Rape*) is perhaps Degas' most sinister and disturbing work and it may be that Degas was reminded of its highly charged mood when he came to paint Michel-Lévy once again.

In this portrait Michel-Lévy is shown against a background of large *plein air* landscape paintings which seem to be in a more or less Impressionist style. Degas' friend and admirer Walter Sickert believed that the picture was intended to be a protest against 'extreme Impressionist tenets' and pointed out that the bonneted female figure in the larger of the two paintings within the picture seemed to have been painted from the figure lying on the floor. It is true that Degas was contemptuous of open air painting and those artists who could only paint from nature were the frequent butt of his sarcasm. Sickert's interpretation of the meaning of the doll is supported by a strange picture entitled *The Doll-Maker*, exhibited at the Salon of 1894 by an artist called Jean Veber. Veber's picture uses similar imagery to promote the opposite viewpoint to that of Degas. A madman stares fixedly at a doll, ignoring a beautiful naked woman beside him. Contemporary critics understood the picture as an attack on those artists who disregard nature.

Michel-Lévy was a minor artist who achieved a modest success at the Salon in the 1880s and is remembered today only for Degas' portrait. Degas broke with him in 1891 when he sold the portrait, which he had exchanged for another which he had made of Degas.

Portrait of Diego Martelli, 1879

110 × 100cm. National Gallery of Scotland, Edinburgh

The portrait of Diego Martelli was first exhibited in the fourth Impressionist exhibition of 1879 along with several other of Degas' finest portraits, including those of Edmond Duranty and Henri Michel-Lévy. Indeed, this exhibition might be seen as the high point of Degas' interest in portraiture. Diego Martelli was an Italian art critic closely associated with the Macchiaioli, a group of artists sometimes seen as Italian forerunners of Impressionism. Martelli came to Paris in the spring of 1878 to the Universal Exhibition and remained over a year, during which time he came to know Degas. At the end of the year he wrote back to a friend in Italy that he was 'running the risk of becoming a friend' of Degas and described him as 'a man of wit and artist of talent who is threatened by blindness . . . and who under such circumstances can be sad and disconsolate.' Martelli was profoundly impressed by the Impressionist exhibition in which his portrait was shown and became one of the earliest propagandists for the new French painting in Italy.

Degas has depicted Martelli in his Paris apartment surrounded by a bohemian disorder of papers indicating Martelli's profession as a writer. Other telling details are the pipe and the scarlet-lined slippers which seem to follow the precept written by Degas in a notebook of the 1870s, 'Draw all kinds of everyday objects placed and accompanied in such a way that they have in them the life of the man or woman.'

In another notebook of around the same time Degas wrote, 'Workshop plans: set up tiers all around the room to get used to drawing things from above and below . . . For a portrait, pose the model on the ground floor and work on the first floor to get used to retaining forms and expressions and never drawing or painting immediately.' This portrait of Diego Martelli is one of the most extreme examples of Degas' predilection at this time for using high viewpoints. This did not find favour with all Degas' friends and followers. The English painter Walter Sickert saw 'a touch of perverseness' in the excessively high viewpoint of Martelli's portrait, adding that 'Degas seems to have gone out of his way to select a bird's-eye view for his portrait, almost because many bad paintings were being done on studio thrones.' It was because Degas' friend Duranty criticized the resultant foreshortening of the legs that Degas refused to allow Martelli to take possession of his portrait.

Dancers in the Wings, c.1880

69 × 48cm. Norton Simon Art Foundation, Pasadena

Degas often seemed to take a perverse delight in setting expectations on their heads and breaking all the rules as laid down by the academic artists of his day. *Dancers in the Wings* is an example of the spirit of radical experimentation which permeated Degas' work in the late 1870s. Upsetting traditional notions of balance and harmony, he creates a disorienting effect by his use of asymmetry and the cutting of the figures (though the asymmetrical placing of the figures is countered by the strong diagonals of the stage flat).

The picture also shows Degas' unconventional approach to the medium of pastel. Having drawn the image in pastel, he reworked areas of it using powdered pastel diluted with water, and added touches of tempera. The opaque medium of pastel allowed him to indulge his passion for making alterations and by working on paper he could alter the size of the image at will by cutting or adding strips. In *Dancers in the Wings*, Degas added eight strips of paper to the central piece.

At the Milliner's, 1882

75.9 × 84.8cm. Thyssen-Bornemisza Collection, Lugano

The series of approximately ten pictures of women trying on hats, mostly executed in pastel, all belong to the early 1880s. They are amongst the most charming of Degas' works and have always been popular, especially with the English and Americans who in the nineteenth century were frequently alarmed by the more equivocal and challenging aspects of his other subjects. *At the Milliner's* was in fact first exhibited in 1882 in London where it was warmly praised by the critic of *The Standard*.

Degas is more interested in this series in capturing the characteristic movement of the arm or the twist of the torso as the women try on hats or look in the mirror, than he is in facial likeness. Faces are either hidden or else rather generalized as with the girl on the right in this picture. Even in this generalized form, it is apparent that the faces of this series have a more refined cast of features than Degas gave to the equally anonymous women in the pictures of dancers, laundresses, café-concert singers and prostitutes. In *At the Milliner's*, the viewer seems to be leaning forward to stare through a shop window from a short distance. The elaborate display of hats provides Degas with interesting shapes to draw and the opportunity to exploit his brilliant pastel technique to the full.

Miss Cassatt, Holding Cards, c.1884

71.5 × 58.7cm. National Portrait Gallery, Washington

Most of the artist friends whom Degas gathered around him and who formed a clique within the Impressionist exhibitions were mediocrities or at best minor talents. The one great exception to this was the American painter, Mary Cassatt. Although she was initially regarded as a follower of Degas and was indeed indebted to him in many ways, she possessed a talent that was strong and individual enough to prove wrong Brancusi's maxim, 'Nothing grows in the shadow of big trees.'

Mary Cassatt was the daughter of a wealthy American businessman of French ancestry. After training at the Pennsylvania Academy of Fine Arts, she set out for Europe and settled in Paris in 1874, the year of the first Impressionist exhibition. After making the acquaintance of Degas in 1877 she took part in four of the last five Impressionist exhibitions, abstaining only from the seventh exhibition from which Degas and his friends were excluded. Their friendship was at its closest in the early 1880s, when Cassatt posed for several of Degas' pastels of milliners and for the etching *At the Louvre*. At this time they were even rumoured to be having an affair. Given Degas' lack of interest in such matters this seems highly unlikely, although it is intriguing that Cassatt later felt it necessary to destroy their correspondence.

Despite his prejudices against women and his loud assertions that they were incapable of understanding art, Degas had a profound admiration for Cassatt's work. In 1886 he acquired her *Girl Arranging her Hair*, which he displayed prominently for many years as one of the glories of his collection.

The sober, even grim character of this portrait could hardly be more different from the relaxed and passive elegance of most nineteenth-century portraits of women. Cassatt's forward-leaning pose, tense as a coiled spring, marvellously conveys the energy and forcefulness of her personality. Her enigmatic gesture in holding out tarot or playing-cards has not been satisfactorily explained, though it has been suggested that the unconventional, perhaps even unseemly gesture for a respectable woman was partly responsible for her later aversion to the picture. After having hung the portrait in her studio for many years she seems to have conceived an intense dislike for it, writing at about the time she sold it, 'I do not wish to leave it to my family as a portrait of me. It has artistic qualities, but is so distressing and represents me as a person so repulsive, that I do not want it known that I posed for it.'

Laundresses, c.1884–86

76 × 81cm. Musée d'Orsay, Paris

On Friday 13 February 1874, the novelist Edmond de Goncourt wrote in his diary, 'Yesterday I spent the afternoon in the studio of a painter named Degas. After a many attempts, many bearings taken in every direction, he has fallen in love with the modern and, in the modern, he has cast his choice upon laundresses and dancers . . . Degas places before our eyes laundresses and more laundresses, while . . . explaining to us technically the downward pressing and the circular strokes of the iron, etc. etc.'

Whether he was depicting bankers, musicians, dancers, jockeys or laundresses, Degas always paid great attention to capturing the characteristic movements and poses of the subject's class and profession.

The picture illustrated here is the most impressive of the four versions of the composition which Degas made over a period of about fifteen years. The powerfully volumetric treatment of the figures is exceptional in his work and probably owes something to the influence of Daumier, from whom Degas had borrowed the subject of laundresses in the first place. The earthy, slightly humorous realism of the picture is also reminiscent of Daumier. Degas was a passionate admirer of Daumier's lithographs and by the end of his life had collected some 1,800 of them.

The technique is also an unusual one for Degas. Instead of the fine canvas which he had favoured up to this time he has used a coarse, unprimed canvas which is allowed to show through in many areas of the picture. The dry and crumbly paint is only dense enough to fill the open pores of the thirsty canvas surface on the highlights of the yawning woman on the left.

The steep diagonal created by the table at which the women work is reminiscent of the kind of perspective found in Japanese prints.

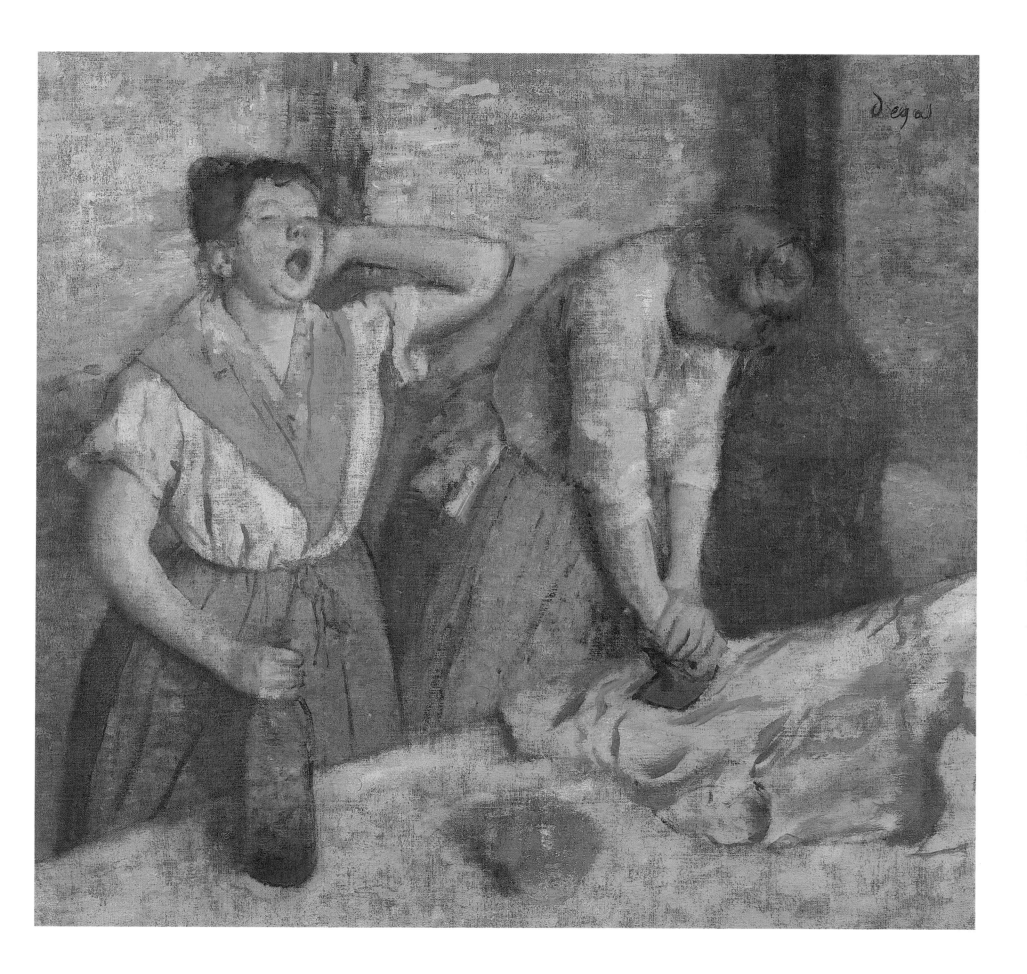

Nude Woman Drying her Foot, c.1885–86

50.2 × 54cm. Metropolitan Museum of Art, New York

Nude Woman Drying her Foot is an example of the awkward and uncomfortable poses that Degas favoured for his nudes in the 1880s. Many of these poses must have been excruciating for the models to hold over any length of time. In this respect there was some element of truth in the accusation of the novelist and critic Joris-Karl Huysmans that Degas' *toilettes* showed a 'lingering cruelty and a patient hatred' towards women.

Despite stories about Degas' irritability with his models and his habit of cross-examining them about their racial origins at the height of the anti-semitism whipped up by the Dreyfus Affair, Degas seems to have built up good relationships with his models, if not the kind of long-lasting affectionate ties that Renoir had with his. The recollections of a model named Alice Michel, who posed for Degas in the final years of his career, give the impression of a tetchy but basically good-natured old man willing to chat and joke with his models while he worked.

Nude Woman Drying her Foot makes an interesting contrast with the nudes painted in the 1890s such as *Sleeping Woman* by Renoir. Renoir's picture, although also ostensibly a bather, is essentially a pin-up; not engaged in washing or drying herself, she assumes a pose calculated to show off the beauty of her body with its firm breasts and luminous pearly skin. The generalized setting does not even make it clear whether the scene is taking place indoors or in the open air.

Degas' model, in a comfortable modern interior with an upholstered armchair, is entirely absorbed in the activity of drying her toes and bent double in a position which precludes any hint of voluptuousness. Her body is that of an ordinary young woman and her slightly sweaty skin has an unhealthy pallor.

$586

Hélène Rouart in her Father's Study, c.1886

161 × 120cm. National Gallery, London

Hélène Rouart was the daughter of the industrialist and art-collector Henri Rouart, with whom Degas had been at school at the Lycée Louis-le-Grand in the years around 1850. Degas and Rouart met again during the Franco-Prussian War in 1870 and remained on terms of closest friendship until the latter's death in 1912. Degas had already painted Rouart in front of his factory and Hélène on her father's knee, in a touching double portrait of the 1870s. Degas was initially tempted by her beautiful colouring to paint another portrait of Hélène as a young woman. In 1883 he wrote to Rouart, who was staying in Venice with his family, 'I should have liked to have come with you and begun the portrait of your daughter, there in Venice, where her hair and colouring are of the kind so much admired in the past.' The following year he wrote, 'Your daughter, who has always had such pretty colouring, must by now be dazzling.' Hélène's lovely colouring determined the golden tonality of the whole painting with the pinkish wall under the reddish orange of the Chinese wall-hanging and objects heavily contoured in warm browns.

As in his portraits of Duranty and Martelli, Degas shows Hélène in the familiar surroundings of her home. However, the objects speak not of her interests and enthusiasms, but of those of her father. With her tentative and slightly melancholy expression (which she also wears in contemporary photographs), Hélène seems hemmed in, almost imprisoned by her father's magnificent possessions. Degas was extraordinarily adept and subtle in indicating the psychological tensions which existed beneath the polite reserve of bourgeois households.

Contemporary photographs of the Rouart family home in the rue de Lisbonne show that the vitrine contained Egyptian objects, although Degas took artistic licence in enlarging the statuettes. The pictures to the right have been identified as a landscape by Corot and a drawing by Millet, both of which belonged to Henri Rouart. The handsome classical chair on which Hélène leans and which acts as a kind of barrier came from the family of Hélène's mother, who was descended from the great *ébéniste*, Jacob Desmalter.

The portrait was never given to the Rouart family but remained in Degas' studio until his death. Bare patches of canvas in the lower part of the picture, visible pentimenti around the shoulders and the unresolved painting of the hands which are so prominently placed in the picture, might suggest that it was never finished, although conventional standards of 'finish' can never be applied to Degas' work.

The Tub, 1886

60 × 83cm. Musée d'Orsay, Paris

The Tub was first shown at the eighth and last Impressionist exhibition in 1886 in a group of pastels to which Degas gave the collective title *Series of Nudes of Women Bathing, Washing, Drying, Rubbing Down, Combing their Hair or Having it Combed.* Although Degas had shown monotypes of similar subjects in the 1870s, this was the first occasion on which he showed an important group of pastels of a subject which was to obsess him for the last twenty-five years of his active career.

Renoir, who was very much preoccupied with the nude at this time and dissatisfied with the Impressionist negation of form and contour, freely admitted to Vollard that Degas' *toilettes* were a revelation to him in the midst of his stylistic experiments. Degas, who had been excluded from the seventh Impressionist show may have noted with satisfaction that the last exhibition clearly marked the demise rather than the triumph of Impressionism. While the arch-Impressionists Monet and Sisley stayed away, the work of the profoundly anti-Impressionist painter Odilon Redon was shown. The hardening of contours and more synthetic approach to form of Gauguin and Pissarro marked a move away from the spontaneous and direct painting from nature of which Degas disapproved. The most important contribution to the exhibition, apart from Degas' *toilettes*, was Seurat's *A Sunday Afternoon on the Island of La Grande Jatte*, a masterpiece which takes some Impressionist tenets to their logical extreme, while at the same time showing a reaction to the more casual and spontaneous aspects of Impressionism and a move towards a more disciplined and monumental style.

In one respect *The Tub* marks the end rather than the beginning of a phase in Degas' work. It is one of Degas' last pictures to show the kind of high viewpoint which so intrigued him in the years around 1880. The extreme asymmetry of the composition, and the startling use of the marble table top with its steep and ambiguous perspective, are examples of the Japanese influence which diminishes in his work from the mid-1880s. From this time onwards, Degas' viewpoints tend to drop to more normal levels. He focuses more closely upon the figure and pays less attention to the surroundings and accessories.

Woman Combing her Hair, c.1890–92

82 × 57cm. Musée d'Orsay, Paris

Many artists and writers of the late nineteenth century had a fascination with women's hair that bordered on fetishism. One of the most extreme in this respect was the Pre-Raphaelite painter and poet Dante Gabriel Rossetti. The novelist Mrs. Gaskell described how when a woman with beautiful hair entered the room he was 'like the cat turned into a lady, who jumped out of bed and ran after a mouse' and concluded that 'he is not as mad as March hare, but hair-mad.'

Women's hair was seen as beautiful and voluptuous, but also as something dangerous – a weapon and a means of entrapping men. Numerous Pre-Raphaelite and Symbolist pictures show men caught up in women's hair. In Art Nouveau images women's hair becomes tentacular and develops a life of its own. The literature of the period too abounds in erotic images of the subject. Pierre Louy's poem *The Hair* (which inspired an exquisite song by Debussy) expresses a claustrophobic sensuality with a hint of threat: 'Last night I dreamed I had your hair around my neck. I had your tresses like a black necklace around my neck and on my chest. I caressed them and they were mine and we were bound together for ever in this way, by the same hair, mouth against mouth, just as two laurel trees have only one root. And gradually it seemed to me, so much were our limbs mingled, that I was becoming yourself or that you were entering into me like my dream.'

The most famous scene in Maurice Maeterlinck's play *Pelléas and Mélisande*, which is exactly contemporary with this pastel, has Mélisande combing her hair out of the window of a castle tower. When her hair falls over Pelleas and completely envelops him he cries out, 'I've never seen hair like yours, Melisande. Look, look how it comes from so high and yet covers me even to my heart; it reaches right to my knees! And it's so soft, as soft as though it fell from heaven. I can't see the sky through your hair . . . you see, you see? My two hands can't hold it all; it flows over the branches of the willow. It lives like birds between my fingers, and it loves me, loves more than you.'

Degas' depictions of women combing their hair have a voluptuous quality quite unparalleled elsewhere in his work and show that he too, like so many of his contemporaries, was deeply fascinated. There are stories of Degas late in his career happily combing the hair of his models for hours on end. Years earlier he had amazed the family of his friend Ludovic Halévy by making a formal request for permission to watch Geneviève Halévy (the widow of the composer Georges Bizet) combing her hair.

Hilly Landscape, c.1890–93

25.4 × 34cm. Metropolitan Museum of Art, New York

Degas' friends and admirers were taken by surprise when he exhibited a series of over twenty colour monotypes of landscapes reworked in pastel. Degas had never shown much interest in landscape and was positively hostile to the kind of open-air landscape painting practised by the Impressionists. To Vollard Degas said, 'You know what I think of people who work out in the open. If I were the government, I would have a special brigade of gendarmes to keep an eye on artists who paint landscapes from nature.' Degas' close friend Henri Rouart, when he painted a landscape out on the cliffs, was reprimanded with the tart comment, 'Painting is not a sport.'

Degas' delicate, poetic and quasi-abstract landscapes have indeed very little to do with the direct transcriptions of nature painted by the Impressionists. In a letter to his sister Marguerite in which he mentioned the exhibition at Durand-Ruel's gallery, Degas stressed that the landscapes were done from his imagination. The illustrator Georges Jeanniot, at whose country house Degas made the monotypes, described how he came to do them, 'The journey had been a marvel to Degas. With his astonishing memory he had noted various aspects of nature which he reconstructed from his recollections during the few days he spent with us. Bartholomé (the sculptor) was astounded to see him drawing the landscapes as though they were still before his eyes, "And you must realize," Bartholomé said, "that not once did he make me stop the carriage in order to have a longer look." '

Jeanniot lent Degas a studio with primitive print-making equipment. 'Once he had everything he needed he set to work without delay, without allowing his attention to be distracted. His fingers were thick, but well shaped. He picked up the different tools, handling them with surprising dexterity, and little by little upon the metal surface there appeared a valley, a sky, some white houses, some black-branched fruit trees, some birches and oaks, ruts full of water from the recent shower, orange-tinted clouds flying across a chequered sky above the red and green landscape . . . Then he asked for pastels to finish the monotypes, and it was at this stage, even more than in preparing the proof, that I admired his taste, his imagination and the vividness of his recollections . . . '

After the Bath, Woman Drying the Nape of her Neck, c.1895

62.2 × 65cm. Musée d'Orsay, Paris

Degas' *toilettes* of the 1890s show a new breadth of conception and a love of large, simple, sculptural volumes. The eighteenth-century historian Johann Winckelmann might have been a little surprised to find his famous catch-phrase applied to such a subject, but one could say that Degas' *toilettes* of this period exhibit the 'noble simplicity and calm grandeur' which characterizes the greatest products of the classical tradition. Renoir, who was seeking and not always finding a similarly noble and timeless quality in his late nudes, recognised the innate classicism of those of Degas, comparing one of them to the frieze of the Parthenon.

The technique of pastel enabled Degas to become, as he himself put it, 'a colourist with line'. It is in these late pastel nudes that Degas realized most completely the synthesis of line and colour which had become the goal of many French artists after the time of Ingres and Delacroix. The dense, iridescent weave of brilliant colour achieves an effect of oriental luxury and splendour and may owe something to the love of oriental carpets which Degas developed around this time. As in virtually all his *toilettes*, Degas preserves the anonymity of his sitter by turning her face away from us.

The Return of the Herd, c.1898

71 × 92cm. Leicestershire Museum and Art Galleries, Leicester

The Return of the Herd belongs to a group of a dozen or so landscapes which Degas painted in oil at the small village of Saint-Valéry-sur-Somme on the channel coast of France around 1898. Degas went there to stay with a wealthy amateur painter, Louis Braquaval, with whom he had recently become friends. It may have been nostalgia for his early childhood, when Degas' parents had brought him to stay in the region, that prompted him to paint landscapes with a greater degree of naturalism and topographical accuracy than his early monotypes, although he continued to use colour in a subjective and arbitrary way. *The Return of the Herd*, which few people would be likely to recognize as the work of Degas, is reminiscent both of the sombre Pre-Impressionist landscapes of the Barbizon School and of the Post-Impressionist Breton landscapes of Gauguin, a younger artist whose work Degas greatly admired and several of whose pictures he owned.

Four Dancers, c.1899

151 × 180cm. National Gallery of Art, Washington

Degas continued to paint and draw dancers until the end of his career, although his style had changed dramatically since the small, cool, immaculately painted canvases of the early 1870s such as *Dance Foyer at the Opera in the Rue le Peletier*. Some of these changes had been forced upon him by encroaching blindness. He now painted on a larger scale, using a broad technique and fierce, almost hallucinatory colours. The dancers, seen from close to, occupy a large part of the picture space. Degas concentrated on the casual gestures of the dancers adjusting the straps of their costumes. The gestures were obviously clearly impressed on Degas' memory as he uses them in different combinations in several pictures of this period. The stylistic changes in his late works also coincide with a general tendency towards a greater subjectivity and degree of abstraction in French avant-garde painting at the end of the century. Degas' best pictures of the 1890s have a heightened and poetic quality which place them among his finest and most personal achievements.

CHRONOLOGY

1834 19th July
Birth of Hilaire Germain Edgar De Gas at 8 rue Saint-Georges, Paris.

1845 October
Enters the Lycée Louis-le-Grand

1847 5th September
Death of Degas' mother.

1853 March
Leaves school.

1853 April
Receives permission to copy in the Louvre.

1853 November
Enrols as a student of law.

1855
Meets Ingres.

1855 April
Registers at the École des Beaux-Arts.

1856 July
Arrives in Naples to stay with relatives.

1856 October
Arrives in Rome to study, and remains, with one interruption, until July 1858.

1858 August –
1859 Spring
Stays in Florence with his Aunt Laure and her husband Baron Bellelli. Begins studies for the portrait of the Bellelli family.

1865
Scene of Warfare in the Middle Ages (The Misfortunes of the Town of Orléans) exhibited at the Paris Salon.

1866
Exhibits a painting of a steeple chase at the Salon.

1867
Exhibits two family portraits at the Salon, one of which was probably *The Bellelli Family.*

1868 May
Exhibits the portrait, *Mlle Fiocre; á propos du ballet de 'La Source'* at the Salon.

1870 May
Exhibits at the Salon for the last time.

1870 19th July
France declares war on Prussia.

1870 September
Degas volunteers for the National Guard.

1871 October
Visits London.

1872 October –
1873 March
Visits relations in New Orleans.

1874 12th February
Edmond de Goncourt visits Degas' studio.

1874 April
First Impressionist exhibition.

1875
Degas sells his art collection to help pay family debts.

1876 30th March
Second Impressionist exhibition opens.

1877 April
Third Impressionist exhibition. Degas exhibits monotypes, pastels and oils.

1879 April
Fourth Impressionist exhibition. Degas exhibits some of his finest works, including *Miss La La at the Cirque Fernando* and the portraits of Duranty and Diego Martelli.

1880 April
Fifth Impressionist exhibition. Degas' exhibits are warmly praised by the novelist Huysmans.

1881
Sixth Impressionst exhibition. Degas exhibits the sculpture *Little Dancer Aged 14.*

1882 March
Degas and his closest associates (including Mary Cassatt) are absent from the Seventh Impressionst exhibition.

1886 May
Eighth and last Impressionist exhibition. Degas exhibits his pastel *toilettes* for the first time.

1890
Degas makes his first landscape monotypes.

1892 September
Degas' first one-man show at Durand-Ruel's gallery, in which he exhibits landscapes.

1893

Absinthe exhibited in London amidst controversy.

1894

Dreyfus condemned to life imprisonment.

1895

Degas buys eight works by Gauguin and Delacroix's portrait of Baron Schwiter.

1896

Seven works by Degas accepted by the Musée du Luxembourg as part of the Caillebotte legacy. Degas buys works by Cézanne and Van Gogh and Ingres' portrait of M. and Mme Leblanc.

1897

As the Dreyfus affair reaches its height, Degas breaks with his Jewish friends, including Ludovic Halévy.

1912

Degas forced to move from the apartment in the rue Victor-Masse where he had lived since 1890. About this time Degas ceases to work.

1917 28th September

Death of Degas.

BIBLIOGRAPHY

ADHEMAR, J. and CACHIN, F. *Edgar Degas, Gravures et monotypes*, catalogue of etchings and lithographs, Paris, 1973.

DUNLOP, I. *Degas*, London, 1979.

LEMOISNE, P.A. *Degas et son œuvre*, catalogue of paintings and pastels, 4 vols. Paris, 1946–49.

REFF, T. *Degas; The Artist's Mind*, London, 1976.

—— *The Notebooks of Edgar Degas*, 2 vols. Oxford, 1976.

REWALD, J. *Degas' Sculpture, The Complete Works*, New York, 1956.

—— *The History of Impressionism*, New York, 1946, re-printed London, Secker and Warburg, 1980.

VOLLARD, A. *Degas*, New York, 1927, re-printed Dover Publications, New York, 1986.

Degas Exhibition Catalogue, Galeries Nationales du Grand Palais, Paris/The Metropolitan Museum of Art, New York, 1988.

LIST OF PLATES

5: Degas, *Little Dancer Aged 14*, 1880–81, bronze, h. 98.4 cm. The Tate Gallery, London.

13: Daumier, *The Orchestra During the Performance of a Tragedy*, 1852, Lithograph, 26.1 × 21.6 cm. Metropolitan Museum of Art, New York.

15: Rossetti, Study of a Woman's Head for *Found*, c1853–57, pen and ink over pencil, 10.5 × 9.2 cm. Birmingham Museum and Art Gallery.

16: Hiroshige, *Ferry at Haneda*, c1858, woodcut print from *One Hundred Views of Edo*, 35.3 × 24 cm. Reproduced by courtesy of the Trustees of the British Museum, London.

17: Yoshitoshi, *A Poem by Abe No Nakamara*, from the series *One Hundred Aspects of the Moon*, 1888, woodcut print, 33 × 22.5 cm. Author's collection.

18: Degas, *Danseuses*, c1879, pastel, 18 × 60 cm. Photo: Archives Durand Ruel, Paris.

20: Degas, *Rehearsal of a Ballet on Stage*, 1874, oil on canvas, 65 × 81 cm. Musée d'Orsay, Paris.

21: Degas, *Two Dancers on the Stage*, 1874, oil on canvas, 61.5 × 64 cm. Courtauld Institute Galleries, London: Courtauld Collection.

21: Béraud, *Backstage at the Opera*, 1889, oil on wood, 32 × 54 cm. Musée Carnavalet, Paris.

22: Degas, *The Curtain*, c1880, pastel over monotype, 35 × 41 cm. Collection of Mr and Mrs Paul Mellon, Upperville, Virginia.

25: Powell Frith, *Derby Day*, 1856–58, oil on canvas, 101.6 × 223.5 cm. The Tate Gallery, London.

27: Holman-Hunt, *The Awakening Conscience*, 1853, oil on canvas, 72.6 × 55.9 cm. The Tate Gallery, London.

28: Degas, *The Serious Client*, c1879, monotype on wove paper, 21 × 15.9 cm. National Gallery of Canada, Ottawa.

29: Degas, *Waiting*, second version, 1876–77, monotype, 21.6 × 16.4 cm. Musée Picasso, Paris.

31: Degas, *Woman Drying Herself*, c1889–90, pastel on paper, 67.7 × 57.8 cm. Courtauld Institute Galleries, London: Courtauld Collection.

32: Renoir, *Reclining Female Nude*, 1897, oil on canvas, 81 × 65.5 cm. Oskar Reinhart Collection, Winterthur, Switzerland.

35: Degas, *Woman Standing in a Bathtub*, c1879–85, monotype, 38 × 27 cm. Musée d'Orsay, Paris.

36: Degas, *After the Bath*, c1896, oil on canvas, 89 × 116 cm. Philadelphia Museum of Art. Purchased: Estate of the late George D. Widener.

37: *After the Bath*, 1896, photograph by Degas. Collection of the J. Paul Getty Museum, Malibu, California.

38: *Apotheosis of Degas*, parody of Ingres' *Apotheosis of Homer*, 1885, photograph. Bibliothèque Nationale, Paris.

39: Degas leaving a public lavatory, 1889, photograph by Count Giuseppe Primoli. Bibliothèque Nationale, Paris.

40: Degas, *Dancer Looking at the Sole of her Foot*, 1910–11, bronze, h. 47.6 cm. The Tate Gallery, London.

41: Degas, *Seated Dancer, View of Profile From the Right*, 1873, drawing à l'essence on blue paper, 23 × 29.2 cm. Cabinet des Dessins, Musée d'Orsay, Paris.

42: Degas in Bartholomé's garden, c1908, photograph by Bartholomé. Bibliothèque Nationale, Paris.

45: *Portrait of the Artist*, 1855, oil on canvas, 81 × 64 cm. Musée d'Orsay, Paris.

47: *Roman Beggar Woman*, 1857, oil on canvas, 100.3 × 75.2 cm. Birmingham Museum and Art Gallery.

49: *Portrait of Hilaire Degas*, 1857, oil on canvas, 53 × 41 cm. Musée d'Orsay, Paris.

51: *The Bellelli Family*, 1858–67, oil on canvas, 200 × 250 cm. Musée d'Orsay, Paris.

53: *Semiramis Building Babylon*, c1860–62, oil on canvas, 150 × 258 cm. Musée d'Orsay, Paris.

55: *Young Spartans*, c1860–62, oil on canvas, 109 × 155 cm. Reproduced by courtesy of the Trustees, The National Gallery, London.

57: *Portrait of the Artist*, c1863, oil on canvas, 92.5 × 66.5 cm. Calouste Gulbenkian Foundation, Lisbon.

59: *Scene of Warfare in the Middle Ages (the Misfortunes of the Town of Orléans)*, 1865, peinture à l'essence on paper on canvas, 81 × 147 cm. Musée d'Orsay, Paris.

61: *Jockeys in Front of the Grandstands*, c1866–68, peinture à l'essence on paper on canvas, 46 × 61 cm. Musée d'Orsay, Paris.

63: *James Tissot in an Artist's Studio*, 1867–68, oil on canvas, 151 × 112 cm. Metropolitan Museum of Art, New York.

65: *M. and Mme. Edouard Manet*, c1868–69, oil on canvas, 65 × 71 cm. Kitakyushu Municipal Museum of Art, Kitakyushu.

67: *Interior*, c1868–69, oil on canvas, 81 × 116 cm. Philadelphia Museum of Art: The Henry P. McIlhenny Collection in memory of Frances P. McIlhenny.

69: *Melancholy*, c1869, oil on canvas, 19 × 24.7 cm. © The Phillips Collection, Washington, D.C.

71: *Sulking*, c1869–71, oil on canvas, 32.4 × 46.4 cm. Metropolitan Museum of Art, New York.

73: *The Orchestra of the Opera*, c1870, oil on canvas, 56.5 × 46.2 cm. Musée d'Orsay, Paris.

75: *Lorenzo Pagans and Auguste De Gas*, c1871–72, oil on canvas, 54 × 40 cm. Musée d'Orsay, Paris.

77: *Dance Foyer at the Opera in the rue Le Peletier*, 1872, oil on canvas, 32 × 46 cm. Musée d'Orsay, Paris.

79: *Woman with an Oriental Vase*, 1872, oil on canvas, 65 × 34 cm. Musée d'Orsay, Paris.

81: *Portraits in an Office, New Orleans*, 1873, oil on canvas, 73 × 92 cm. Musée des Beaux-Arts, Pau.

83: *The Pedicure*, 1873, oil on canvas, 61 × 46 cm. Musée d'Orsay, Paris.

85: *Rehearsal of a Ballet on Stage*, 1874, peinture à l'essence on paper on canvas, 54.3 × 73 cm. Metropolitan Museum of Art, New York. Gift of Horace Havemeyer, 1929. The H.O. Havemeyer Collection.

87: *The Dance Class*, 1873–75, peinture à l'essence on paper on canvas, 85 × 75 cm. Musée d'Orsay, Paris.

89: *Absinthe*, 1875–76, oil on canvas, 92 × 68 cm. Musée d'Orsay, Paris.

91: *Aux Ambassadeurs*, c1876, pastel on monotype, 37 × 27 cm. Musée des Beaux-Arts, Lyon.

93: *At the Races, Gentlemen Jockeys*, 1876, finished 1887, oil on canvas, 66 × 81 cm. Musée d'Orsay, Paris.

95: *Ballet Scene from 'Robert the Devil'*, 1876, oil on canvas, 76.6 × 81.3 cm. By courtesy of the Board of Trustees of the Victoria and Albert Museum, London.

97: *The Star*, 1876–77, pastel on monotype, 58 × 42 cm. Musée d'Orsay, Paris.

99: *The Madame's Birthday*, 1876–77, pastel on monotype, 26.6 × 29.6 cm. Musée Picasso, Paris.

101: *On the Beach*, 1876–77, oil on paper on canvas, 47 × 82.6 cm. Reproduced by courtesy of the Trustees, The National Gallery, London.

103: *Dancer with a Bouquet*, c1877, pastel over monotype, 40.3 × 50.4 cm. Museum of Art, Rhode Island School of Design, Providence. Gift of Mrs Murray S. Danforth.

105: *Women on a Café Terrace, Evening*, 1877, pastel on monotype, 41 × 60 cm. Musée d'Orsay, Paris.

107: *The Glove*, c1878, pastel and liquid medium on canvas, 52.8 × 41.1 cm. Courtesy of the Fogg Art Museum, Harvard University, Cambridge, Massachussetts, Bequest of Collection of Maurice Wertheim, Class of 1906.

109: *Jockeys Before the Start*, c1878–80, oil on paper, 107.3 × 73.7 cm. The Barber Institute of Fine Arts, the University, Birmingham.

111: *Miss La La at the Cirque Fernando*, 1879, oil on canvas, 117 × 77.5 cm. Reproduced by courtesy of the Trustees, The National Gallery, London.

113: *Portrait of Henri Michel-Lévy*, 1879, oil on canvas, 41.5 × 27.3 cm. Calouste Gulbenkian Foundation, Lisbon.

115: *Portrait of Diego Martelli*, 1879, oil on canvas, 110 × 100 cm. National Gallery of Scotland, Edinburgh.

117: *Dancers in the Wings*, c1880, pastel and tempera on paper on card, 43.8 × 50 cm. Norton Simon Art Foundation, Pasadena.

119: *At the Milliner's*, 1882, pastel, 75.9 × 84.8 cm. Thyssen-Bornemisza Collection, Lugano, Switzerland.

121: *Miss Cassatt, Holding Cards*, c1884, oil on canvas, 71.5 × 58.7 cm. National Portrait Gallery, Smithsonian Institution, Washington. Gift of the Morris and Gwendolyn Cafritz Foundation and the Regent's Major Acquisitions Fund, Smithsonian Institution.

123: *Laundresses*, c1884–86, oil on canvas, 76 × 81 cm. Musée d'Orsay, Paris.

125: *Nude Woman Drying her Foot*, c1885–86, pastel on paper on card, 50.2 × 54 cm. Metropolitan Museum of Art, New York.

127: *Hélène Rouart in her Father's Study*, 1886, oil on canvas, 161 × 120 cm. Reproduced by courtesy of the Trustees, The National Gallery, London.

129: *The Tub*, 1886, pastel on card, 60 × 83 cm. Musée d'Orsay, Paris.

131: *Woman Combing her Hair*, c1890–92, pastel on beige paper on card, 82 × 57 cm. Musée d'Orsay, Paris.

133: *Hilly Landscape*, 1890–93, monotype in oil and pastel, 25.4 × 34 cm. Metropolitan Museum of Art, New York. Purchase, Mr and Mrs Richard J. Bernhard Gift, 1972.

135: *After the Bath, Woman Drying the Nape of her Neck*, c1895, pastel on card, 62.2 × 65 cm. Musée d'Orsay, Paris.

137: *The Return of the Herd*, c1898, oil on canvas, 71 × 92 cm. Leicestershire Museums, Arts and Records Service, Leicester.

139: *Four Dancers*, c1899, 151 × 180 cm. National Gallery of Art, Washington, Chester Dale Collection.

PHOTOGRAPH CREDITS

WITHDRAWN